THE G

THREE EARLY BIOGRAPHIES
OF SPINOZA

BY

PIERRE BAYLE,

JEAN MAXIMILIEN LUCAS,

AND

JOHANNES COLERUS

TRANSLATED BY

KIRK WATSON

2014 (REVISED IN 2018)

Contents

TRANSLATOR'S INTRODUCTION

The philosopher Benedict de Spinoza (1632-77) has been widely praised for his exemplary life: one of integrity, courage, and constancy. To read his biography is to find example after example of how to do the right thing: utter honesty and frugality in everyday dealings, bravely facing angry mobs, refusal to sell out at any price, and keeping strong through suffering, poverty, and illness.

The title of this book is misleading, since Spinoza always insisted that he was not an atheist. However, there is something close to consensus, both from his orthodox opponents and from his atheist fans, that he really does deserve the title, for better or worse. The disagreement pivots on whether the God he believed in truly deserves the name "God"; his "infinite" God is really nothing but nature, reality, or all of existence itself, and therefore his use of the word "God" is superfluous and misleading.

His legacy has been controversial, and it was fought over quite publicly at the end of the 17th century; the biographies in this book show what a provocative and paradoxical figure he had become. The first biography collected here was written by Pierre Bayle

(1647-1706), the famous French author of the *Historical and Critical Dictionary* (1697) and *Thoughts on the Comet* (1682). Bayle, as open-minded and skeptical as he was, was nevertheless a Calvinist and quite hostile to Spinoza's teachings. He considered Spinoza "impious" and called his ideas both "absurd" and "monstrous", but in his *Dictionary* he presented the truth about historical personalities: "I have no right to portray people as I might wish them to have been; I must show how they really were: I can suppress neither their failings nor their virtues." Spinoza is shown in a generally positive light, with regard to his way of life— note that Bayle was also one of the first modern authors to suggest, in comments he added to a later edition of his *Dictionary*, that in history, "the most wicked men were not atheists, while the majority of those atheists whose names have come down to us were good men"[1].

The next early biography was written by one of Spinoza's supporters, Jean Maximilien Lucas (1646-97), a French Protestant refugee who lived in Holland. His is the only fully sympathetic early biography of Spinoza, indeed it verges on hagiography, suggesting that the reader should follow Spinoza's example and keep his teachings in mind at all times. It aims to show how well Spinoza

---

[1] Quotations are from Vol. 15 in the 1820 French edition of the *Dictionary*, pages 272-8.

handled himself in a variety of difficult situations and to contrast the virtues of this "true savant" with many "false savants" in the world, especially the clergy of all religions.

The final biography included here was written by Johannes Colerus, or Johan Köhler (1647-1707), a Lutheran minister who inherited the parish in The Hague where Spinoza spent his final years. It is the most complete early account of Spinoza's life. He gleaned biographical information from interviews with Spinoza's friends and acquaintances and from every document he could lay his hands on, including account-books and letters. He shows great appreciation for the character of his subject—his integrity, frugality, lack of interest in wealth, and his thoroughly sober form of life. But, as with Bayle, this admiration is coupled with an utter abhorrence for everything Spinoza taught about God, the Bible, the soul, church and state relations, and so on.

This collection would be a good supplement to the works and biographies of Spinoza. My intention in translating and preparing them here is to share these fascinating texts with those who love to drink from the sources, to read early and primary documents for themselves. While re-reading this book in early 2018 (in anticipation of a visit to The Netherlands), I noticed and corrected a number of errors, including place-names and spelling mistakes.

SPINOZA

BY PIERRE BAYLE

From THE HISTORICAL AND CRITICAL DICTIONARY, 1697

SPINOZA (Benedict de). This man, a Jew by birth, but an eventual deserter of Judaism who became an atheist in the end, was from Amsterdam. His philosophy was atheistic; and while his was a completely novel system, yet his basic beliefs were shared with many other ancient and modern philosophers, both Western and Eastern. With regard to the latter, you need only read the note in my article "Japan", and what I've written elsewhere about the theology of a certain Chinese sect.

I have been unable to learn anything about the Spinoza family; but we may assume that his origins were in poverty and obscurity. He studied Latin under a medical doctor who was teaching in Amsterdam, and devoted himself to theology, spending many years in its study; after which he turned entirely to philosophy. Being endowed with a geometrical mind, he pursued rationality in all things; therefore, he quickly realized that the teachings of the

8

Rabbis was unsuitable: it is easy to see why he disapproved of many of Judaism's tenets, for his conscience could not bear any restraint, and he hated false appearances: he openly declared what he believed and what he did not. It is said that the Jews offered to tolerate him, provided that he would adhere to their rites; it is even said they offered him a stipend in return for his compliance; but he would have no part in this sort of hypocrisy. For all that, he only gradually distanced himself from their synagogue; he may have stayed even longer with them, if upon leaving the theater one day a Jew had not treacherously stabbed him. The wound was slight, but he took the man's intention to be fatal. After that incident he severed all ties with them, and this led to his excommunication. I have tried to get any details about the related circumstances, but my efforts have been fruitless. He wrote a Defense of his departure from the synagogue in Spanish. This was never published; however, it is thought that it contained many points which were later reproduced in his *Theologico-Political Treatise*, printed in Amsterdam in 1670: a pernicious and detestable book, hinting at the atheism which was later displayed openly in his *Opera Posthuma*. Jean Baptiste Stoupe was wrong to insult the minsters of Holland for failing to respond to the *Theologico-Political Treatise*; he is not always right on that issue.

Spinoza, having turned to philosophical studies, quickly got fed up with philosophy, but then by some miracle he found his salvation in Descartes. He felt such a strong drive for the truth that he renounced the world in a certain fashion, the better to pursue his quest. He was not content to remove himself from all sorts of worldly business: he also abandoned Amsterdam when he found that his friends' frequent visits were hampering his speculations. In search of room to think, he retired to the country, where he also worked on microscopes and telescopes. He continued this life after moving to The Hague; and his highest pleasure was to think, to write his meditations down, and to communicate them to his friends; so, he took little rest, and sometimes three whole months would pass without his setting foot outside his own house. Living in this secluded fashion did not prevent his name and reputation from being widely broadcast, however. Intellectuals came to see him from all parts. The Palatine court asked for him and offered him a chair in philosophy at Heidelberg. He refused the job as being incompatible with his desire to seek after truth without interruption. He fell victim to a slow-acting malady and died in The Hague on February 21st, 1677, at just over forty-four years of age. I understand that the Prince of Condé requested a visit from him while he was in Utrecht in 1673. Spinoza's acquaintances, and the inhabitants of the village where he lived in retirement for some time, all agree that he was an outgoing and affable man, a man of integrity and good manners, and of very good morals.

That may be hard to believe, but we should really not be any more shocked by this than to know that other people conduct their lives very badly, although they believe every word in the Bible. Some claim that he followed the saying, *Nemo repente turpissimus* ("Nobody becomes wicked all at once"), and that he only gradually became an atheist: he was far from it in 1663 when he published his book *A Geometrical Demonstration of the Principles of Descartes*. In this book he is as orthodox on the nature of God as Descartes himself was; but we must remember that he was not sharing his real views in this book. We would be right to think that it was his misuse of some of that philosopher's sayings that led him to the brink. Some think that the anonymous book *De Jure Ecclesiasticorum*, which was printed in 1665, was written by Spinoza as a precursor to his *Theologico-Political Treatise*. Everyone who has refuted the latter has found in it the seeds of atheism; but in this nobody has surpassed Johannes Bredenburg.

It is less easy to resolve all the problems he raises in this book than it is to destroy, root and branch, the system presented in his *Opera Posthuma*; for it is the most monstrous hypothesis imaginable, the most absurd and the most diametrically opposed to the plainest notions that our minds convey to us. It may be said that Providence punished the audacity of this author quite suitably by blinding him in

11

such a way that, in fleeing the difficulties that give a philosopher migraines, he stumbled into quagmires that were infinitely harder to get out of, and so plain to see that no right-thinking person ever mistook them for anything else. Those who complain that the writers who have undertaken to refute him have failed to do it, have confused things: they demand solutions to each of the problems he raised, but they should be content merely to see his presuppositions completely refuted, and the least of his enemies has found that easy to do.

We must not forget that this impious man did not grasp the inevitable dependencies of his system; for he laughed at the idea of spiritual entities, while no philosopher ever had less of a right to deny them. He should have recognized that everything in nature thinks, and that man, as a modification of the universe, is no more enlightened or intelligent than anything else. For this reason, he should have accepted the reality of demons. Everything that his partisans say about miracles is only word-games, which shows all the more how loose and inexact his ideas really are. He died, it is said, as a fully persuaded atheist, and he took precautions to ensure that his reputation as an unbeliever would not be questioned after his death. But, had he reasoned properly, he would not have treated the fear of Hell as illusory. His friends claim that, due to his modesty, he requested that his name should never be applied to any sect.

It is true that his followers are found in large numbers; not many people are suspected of adhering to his teachings: among these, few have studied his works; even fewer of these have understood them, and not been repelled by the difficulties and the impenetrable abstractions found in them. But here's the truth: generally speaking, we call everyone a Spinozist who follows no religion, and who makes little effort to hide it. In the same way, in France we call anyone who seems not to accept the mysteries of the Gospel a Socinian, although most of them have never read the books written either by Sozzini or any of his disciples. The same thing has occurred with Spinoza, and the same thing is inevitable for anyone who creates a system of impiety: they are able to dodge certain objections, but they are exposed to other difficulties, which are far more damaging. If they cannot submit to orthodoxy, if they love to argue so much, it would be more comfortable if they refrained from being so dogmatic. But among all the different atheistic theories, that of Spinoza is the easiest to see through; for, as I have already said, it contradicts the most plain and basic ideas in our heads. A mob of objections rise at once to oppose him, and his responses are even more obscure than the thesis he is trying to maintain—so we may say that his poison carries its own antidote. He would have been fearsome if he had put all his powers to use in clarifying a certain belief that is in fashion in China, and far from what I mentioned in a note I've written on this article.

I just learned something curious: that since he renounced Judaism, he openly professed the Gospel and was a frequent attendee at the assemblies of the Mennonites, or the Arminians, in Amsterdam. He even approved of a confession of faith that one of his close friends shared with him.

What is said of him in the book *Suite du Ménagiana* is so false that I am shocked that Mr. Ménage's friends have not picked up on it. Mr. de Vigneul-Marville would have made them take it out if he had had a hand in the publication of the book; for he has publicly shown that *there is reason to doubt the veracity of this allegation*. His reasons for these doubts are quite astute. His argument fares no better than if he had argued the opposite with an air of certainty. We will discuss another mistake on the same page in that book, elsewhere.

Let us say something about the objections that I have raised against Spinoza's system. I would add a great deal else, if I didn't think it would make this article too long to include in my *Dictionary*: this is not the place to engage in the full debate; I will be content to share a few general observations which attack the foundations of Spinozism and reveal it is a system built on such strange assumptions as to challenge most of the common notions which serve as general rules for philosophical discussion. To fight this system by its opposition to the most obvious and universal axioms that have been common currency in the past, is no doubt a very good way to proceed, although it may have less purchase with hardened Spinozists, than to show them that Spinoza's propositions are contradictory. They could be let off the hook somewhat if they had to concede that his writings were not always consistent; that his proofs are lacking; that he passes over some things that require proof; that his conclusions are wrong, etc. This method, of attacking the absolute faults in his philosophy, and the relative faults of its different parts, has already been done very well in some of the books that set out to refute him. I hear that the author of a short Flemish book printed only a few days ago uses this method with great force and skill.

But to get on to the extra information that I wanted to share: I want to clarify the objection I have raised, regarding the immutability of God. Are the rumors true, and have I misunderstood Spinoza? That would be very strange indeed, since I have only tried to refute the proposition at the basis of his system, which he expresses more clearly than anyone else. I limit myself to fighting against that which he established plainly and precisely as his first principle; that is, that God is the only substance that exists in the universe, and that all other beings are only modifications of this substance. If we fail to understand what he meant by that, it is, no doubt, because he has added novel meanings to these words, without notifying his readers about it. That's a good way to make yourself unintelligible.

Probably the most glaring example of a term that he has taken in a totally novel sense, it is probably *modification*. Whatever he himself understands by this term, his readers will necessarily be confused. I will explore this later, elsewhere. Anyone who reads my objections will easily see that I have taken the word *modality* in its usual sense, and that the consequences I have drawn from it, along with my methodology, are well within the bounds of the normal rules of debate. I assume all readers know where I have attacked him—it has always seemed to me the weakest part of his system, although the Spinozists take least interest in defending him on that point.

I conclude by observing that I have been often told that his doctrine, aside from any religious considerations, appears to be despised by our great mathematicians. This will be easier to understand in light of two things: first, that nobody will be more certain of the multiplicity of substances than those who study spatial extension; second, that most of these good people believe in the reality of the void. Yet, nothing is more opposed to Spinoza's theories than to say that all bodies do not come into contact; and never were two systems more at odds than his and that of the atomists. He agrees with Epicurus that we should reject the idea of Providence, but in everything else their systems harmonize as well as fire and water.

I have recently read a letter where it is related that he spent some time in the city of Ulm, whose magistrate had him exiled because he had spread his pernicious doctrines there, and that it is where he began to write his *Theologico-Political Treatise*. I doubt this very much. The author of the letter adds that his father, in the time when he was still a Protestant, was very a close friend of Spinoza's, and it was by his assistance principally that this rare genius abandoned the Jewish faith.

THE LIFE OF BENEDICT DE SPINOZA

JEAN MAXIMILLIEN LUCAS

1735

We live in very enlightened times, but we still fail to appreciate our outstanding individuals. Although they give us our most important and useful ideas, we hesitate to praise them, either from envy or ignorance; and how surprising it is that, in order to write a biography of one such individual, I have to lay low like a criminal. When such outstanding individuals earned their fame by extraordinary ways, which most people don't know about, then under guise of honoring the established opinions—however absurd and ridiculous these might be—this ignorance will be defended, and to this effect the soundest lights of reason will be sacrificed, along with truth itself. But whatever the risks of this thorny undertaking, I would have learned nothing from the philosophy of the man whose life and principles I am about to set down, if I shrunk from this task from fear. I have little concern for any public outcry, since I have the honor of living in a republic, which allows its subjects the liberty of their opinions, and where the mere desire for happiness and tranquility would be null and void if those whose integrity has been tried, were accepted without jealousy. If this work, which I consecrate to the memory of an illustrious friend, is not approved by everyone, it will be approved at least by those who love the Truth, and who feel the least aversion for the crude and common masses.

Baruch de Spinoza was from Amsterdam, the finest city of Europe, and there was nothing extraordinary about his birth. His father, who was a Jew by religion, and Portuguese by nation, lacked the means to set him up in business, and arranged to have him taught Hebrew instead. This course of study, which included all the learning of the Jews, was not enough to satisfy a mind as brilliant as his. Before he was fifteen years old he had already run up against the harder points which the most learned Jews had long since been debating; and although he was not yet at the age of discernment, yet he was smart enough to see that the questions he was asking were upsetting to his tutor. Wanting to keep out of trouble, he pretended to be wholly satisfied with the responses he received, contenting himself with writing down his concerns, to explore them in their due time and place.

Since the Bible was his only text, soon he was able to stand on his own two feet, having no need of any further instruction. When he started to give his own interpretations, they were so well-grounded that the Rabbis saw that they had been bested on the intellectual plane, and like bullies they resorted to accusations of impiety.

Such bizarre proceedings showed him that he would be unable to pursue the truth in these surroundings: *the masses are wholly ignorant of the truth*; he said, *and to believe the Canonical Books blindly, is to love ancient errors too much*. He resolved to consult no-one else in the future, and that he would spare no effort in this search for the truth. What immense intelligence and extraordinary power of mind it took for him—not yet twenty years old—to devise such an important plan for himself. And he gave early signs that he nothing was being done rashly; he started from the beginning: while reading the Scriptures, he noted their obscure parts, explored their mysteries, and thus pursued his quest beyond those clouds where the Truth was rumored to be hidden.

After his analysis of the Bible, he read and reread the Talmud with the same precision; finding no rival in his comprehension of Hebrew, he found nothing there that was either difficult, nor anything that gave him satisfaction: furthermore, he was careful enough to let his thoughts mature before judging what they were worth.

Now Morteira, a famous Jew, and the least ignorant of the Rabbis of his day, admired the conduct and genius of his disciple. He could not understand how a young man could be so modest when he was possessed of so much understanding. He tested him in every way, to see what he was made of, and later he affirmed that he had found nothing lacking, either in his behavior, or in the beauty of his intellect. Morteira's approval increased his disciple's good reputation, but it did not lead to any vanity. Although he was young, he was mature in his prudence, and had little concern whether other people loved and praised him.

Moreover, his love of truth was so dominant a passion with him, that he had little time left to interact with anyone. But, no matter what precautions he took to keep out of the way, there were times when it cannot be prudently avoided, as noxious as it may be.

Among those who were eager to make his acquaintance, two young men came to see him, ingratiating themselves with him, and begging him to share his true opinions with them. They told him that whatever these were, he had nothing to fear from them, since their curiosity had no goal except to clear up their own doubts.

The young disciple, astonished by such an unexpected request, hesitated a long time before responding; but in the end, pressed by their impatience, he said with a smile, that *Moses and the Prophets were true Israelites*, and that *they gave the final word on all points*; that they should obey these men without hesitation, if they too wanted to be true Israelites.

"When I stick to their writings," replied one of these young men, "I can't find anything about any immaterial existence, nor that God is incorporeal, nor that the soul is immortal, nor that the angels are real substances; what do you think about these things?" he continued, addressing our Disciple. "Does God have a body? Are angels real? Is the soul immortal?"

I affirm, said the Disciple, *that since I find nothing about immateriality or incorporeality in the Bible, there is nothing wrong with believing that God is corporeal, and all the more that God, being great, as the prophet-king said* (Psalms 98:1), *it is impossible to understand any greatness that has no physical dimensions, and which consequently, is not corporeal. As for spirits: it is certain that the Scriptures say nothing about them being real and permanent substances, but that they are simple phantoms called angels, because God uses these to declare His will. Therefore, angels and all other kinds of spirits are only invisible by reason of their very subtle and diaphanous matter, which can only be seen the way you see a phantom: in a mirror, in a dream, or in the dark. In the same way, Jacob was sleeping when he saw angels going up and down on a staircase. This is why we do not find that the Jews excommunicated the Sadducees for not believing in angels, because the Old Testament says nothing about their creation. As for the soul: everywhere the*

Scriptures mention it, the word "soul" is used simply to express the life-force, that is, to designate everything that has life. It would be useless to go looking there for anything to support a belief in immortality. On the contrary, it is plainly stated throughout the book, and nothing could be easier than to prove this: but now is neither the time nor the place to speak about it.

"Well, the little you have said," replied one of the two friends, "would convince anyone; but it is not enough to satisfy us, your friends: we need something stronger, since the matter is too important to not be discussed. We won't leave until you tell us more about these things."

The Disciple, who had been looking for a way to break off the conversation, promised to give them complete satisfaction. But in the ensuing conversation, he carefully avoided every opportunity for them to start down the same track again; and conscious that curiosity rarely has good intentions, he studied the conduct of his 'friends'. He saw so many red flags that he broke off the discussion, trying to get rid of them.

His friends, noting his resolve, contented themselves by murmuring to themselves, still believing that he was only trying their perseverance; but when they saw they had no chance of changing his mind, they swore they would take revenge on him; and to carry it off all the better they defamed him with the masses. They said that it was absurd to believe that this young man might one day become one of the pillars of the Synagogue, and that he would more likely be its destroyer, since he only felt hatred and loathing for the Law of Moses; that they had visited him on Morteira's recommendation; but in the end they had recognized that he was in fact very heterodox; that the Rabbi, as capable as he may be, was wrong about him—indeed, he was gravely mistaken if he had such a good opinion of him, and, finally, his manner horrified them.

This false rumor, although sown at first in secret, soon became very public; and when they saw an opportunity to spread it further, they pressed their case to the elders of the synagogue, who got so worked up by it that, without giving him a chance to plead his defense, quickly judged him guilty.

Once the heat of this first fire spread outward (for the holy ministers of the temple are not more exempt from anger than anyone else), they summoned him before them. He had a clear conscience, and went gladly to the synagogue, where his judges told him with a grave face, and as it were, "consumed with zeal for the house of God", that after the good hopes they had formed of his piety, they had found the evil rumors hard to believe, that they had summoned him to find out the truth, and it was a bitter pill for them to have to summon him to clarify the state of his faith; that he was accused of the blackest and most enormous of all crimes, that is, despising the Law; they earnestly pleaded that he might wash himself clean of it, but they warned that if he was convicted, then no punishment would be too harsh for him.

They asked him how he pleaded, and when they saw that he denied it, his so-called friends, who were standing there present, came forward and brazenly testified that he had mocked that "the Jews as a superstitious people, born and raised in ignorance, who ignored even what God was, and who nevertheless have the audacity to call themselves His people, to the detriment of all other nations. That as for the Law, it had been instituted by a man who was simply more clever than his fellows in political affairs, but who was by no means better informed than they were about the world, or even about God; that an ounce of common sense was enough to show him to be a charlatan, and that you would have to be as stupid as the Hebrews in the days of Moses to praise that particular gentleman." When his accusers added what he had said about God, angels and the soul, the affair really gave them a start: they shouted "Anathema!" before the accused had his turn on the stand.

These judges, moved by a holy zeal to avenge their profaned Law, proceeded to interrogate him. They pressed, threatened, and otherwise tried to intimidate him. But to all this the accused replied nothing, except to say that their manner was pitiable, and that with witnesses like those, he would confirm their testimony, if only compelling arguments could be found.

Now, Morteira, having been warned of the danger his disciple was in, ran immediately to the synagogue where, having taking his place with the judges, he asked them whether he had forgotten the good examples he had been shown, and whether all the work he had put into his education deserved a mutiny like this. He asked whether he was afraid to fall into the hands of the living God. He said that the scandal was already great, but that there was still time for repentance.

When Morteira had exhausted his rhetorical skills without seeing any change in his disciple's attitude, he adopted an angrier tone, and as leader of the synagogue he insisted that he would now have to choose between repentance or punishment, and he threatened him with excommunication.

His disciple calmly responded that he understood the gravity of the threat, and said that as a reward for all the pains he had taken to learn his Hebrew so well, that he now wanted to teach him the formula of excommunication. At these words the Rabbi angrily spews all his bile against him, and after several cold rebukes, he breaks up the assembly, leaves the synagogue, and swears that he will return armed with thunderbolts. But in spite of these threats, he did not expect his disciple to actually wait for him to come back. Of course, he was wrong there; for if he was well informed of the beauty of his disciple's mind, he was ignorant of the force of his character. Since all their threats had fallen on deaf ears, they decided to proceed with his excommunication.

Once he learned about this, he thought it best to withdraw; and far from being frightened, said: "It's a good time for it," he told the person who brought him the news, "I won't be forced into anything, which I won't do myself, if I had no fear of scandal: but since they will have it like this, I joyfully enter the path that is offered to me, with this consolation, that I will be more blameless in my exodus than the first Hebrews were when they were led out of Egypt. However, I won't start off as wealthy as they did, since I'm not making off with anybody's goods. Whatever injustice is done to me, at least I can boast that I've done nothing wrong."

After a while, his interaction with other Jews was reduced virtually to nil, and so he was obliged to get along with the Christians. He had contracted a friendship with certain men of intelligence, and they told him what a pity it was that he knew neither Greek, nor Latin, even though he was already well-versed in Hebrew, Italian, and Spanish, without mentioning German, Flemish and Portuguese, which were his native languages.

He himself felt his lack of these learned tongues; the first obstacle was to find some way of learning them, while being neither wealthy, nor a nobleman, nor having any patron to help him.

Since he was incessantly pondering these things, and constantly speaking about the subject, Van Den Enden, who was a tutor in Greek and Latin, offered his assistance and home, while asking nothing except to share, in time, the burden of teaching his students.

However, Morteira, now very angry at the loathing that his disciple had shown both him and the Law, let his friendship morph into hatred, and delighted in antagonizing him with all the pleasure that mean souls find in vengeance.

The Jewish form of excommunication has nothing novel about it; however, to omit nothing which might be useful for the reader, I will touch on the basic circumstances involved.

After the congregation has gathered in the synagogue, this ceremony, which they call *Cherem*, begins with the lighting of numerous black candles, and opening the tabernacle where the books of the Law are kept. Next, the cantor, in an elevated section, intones with a lugubrious voice the words of execration, while another cantor blows on a horn, and the candles are upturned, making them drip into a vessel full of blood. At this spectacle the congregation, excited by a holy terror and a sacred rage, repeat the word "Amen" with a savage tone, as a sign of the service they believe they thereby render to God, if it caused any pain to the excommunicated one, which it would no doubt do, if he were present for the occasion, or was leaving the Synagogue.

On which point it must be noted that the sound of the horn, the overturned candles and the vessel full of blood, are the circumstances that are only observed in cases of blasphemy, and in other cases they are content to fulminate the excommunication, as was practiced in the case of Spinoza, who was not convicted of blasphemy, but only of having lacked due respect for Moses and the Law.

Excommunication carries such weight with the Jews that the best friends of those who suffer it will not dare do offer him the least service, nor even to speak with them, lest they fall under the same condemnation. Thus, those who fear sweet solitude and the rage of the masses would prefer any punishment to the anathema.

However, Spinoza had now found safe haven, where he felt sheltered from the insults of the Jews, and now only intended to advance further in his studies, where, with as gifted a mind as he had, he expected immense progress in the short term. However, the Jews, both disturbed and upset at having failed in their attack and seeing that their intended victim was now beyond their reach, charged him with a crime which they could not convict him of. I mean the Jews in general; for although those whose livelihood comes from the altar never forgive anyone, yet I won't claim that Morteira and his colleagues were the only accusers on this occasion.

Removing himself beyond their jurisdiction and getting along fine without their support, were two crimes that seemed irredeemable to them. Morteira, above all, could not bear to see his disciple carrying on in the same city, after the grave insult that he thought he had received from him. But how could he drive him away? He was not the leader of the city, as he was of the synagogue; however, malice is so powerful, in the shadow of false zeal, that this old man found a way to do it. Here is what he did: he was escorted by a rabbi of the same temper, and went to the magistrate, explaining to him that he had excommunicated Spinoza, and not for ordinary reasons, but for execrable blasphemies against both Moses and God. He exaggerated the imposture by all the arguments that a holy hatred might suggest to an irreconcilable heart, and demanded that Spinoza be exiled from Amsterdam.

Seeing how carried away the Rabbi was, and

with what fury he declaimed against his disciple, it was easy to judge that it was less a pious zeal than a secret grudge that excited him to this revenge. The judges, noticing this, evaded the matter by referring them onward to the ministers.

The latter, having examined the affair, found themselves overwhelmed. They could find no impiety in the accused when he defended himself; on the other hand, the accuser was a Rabbi, and his rank compelled them remember their own. So that, all things considered, they could not consent to forgive a man whom their colleague wanted rid of, without bringing discord into the ministry; and this reason, for better or worse, led to their conclusion in favor of the Rabbi. So true is it that the ecclesiastics of whatever religion—be they Gentiles, Jews, Christians, or Muslims— are always more concerned about the state of their own authority than about equity and truth, and they are all animated by the same spirit of persecution.

The magistrates, who didn't dare to recant for obvious reasons, condemned the accused to an exile of several months.

By this means Rabbinism was avenged: but it was less because of the will of the judges, than to quiet the unwelcome clamor of the more wearisome and bad-tempered members of the people. Moreover, this arrest, far from being an annoyance to Spinoza, it rather encouraged the desire he had been nurturing to leave Amsterdam.

Having mastered the humanities, which is requisite for a real philosopher, he next sought to get away from the masses of the big city, where people could easily come to disturb his peace: by no means was it persecution which drove him away, but rather the love of solitude, where he had no doubt but that he would find the truth.

This strong and unrelenting passion caused him to depart from his native city with delight, in and he moved to a village called Rijnsburg where, far from all the obstacles presented by life in the city, he devoted himself completely to philosophy. Since he most books were not to his taste, he passed the time thinking his own thoughts instead, having resolved to test them ruthlessly; he had such faith in his own intelligence, and to be sure, few people have understood the world as well as he did.

He spent two years in this retreat, where he had sought to avoid seeing anyone, and his closest friends who did manage to see him from time to time, only left him reluctantly.

Most of his friends were Cartesians, suggested philosophical problems to him which they claimed were insoluble except by the principles of their Master. Spinoza, however, had responses ready for their most perplexing problems, and satisfied them using completely different arguments. So, let us admire both the intelligence of our man and the power of prejudice: these friends returned home stunned, and spread the word that Descartes was not the only philosopher worth following.

Most of the ministers of the day, preoccupied by the doctrine of this great genius, and jealous of their supposed right to infallibility, decry anything anyone says that offends them, and use every means to nip it in the bud. But whatever they did, the evil grows in such a way that, when on the point of a civil war in the empire of letters, when it was stopped and our philosopher was implored to explain himself plainly with regard to Descartes. Spinoza, who only wanted peace, willingly spent a few hours of his free time to this task, and had it printed in 1663.

In this work he proved, geometrically, the two first parts of the *Principles* of Descartes, which he explains in the preface, from the pen of one of his friends. But although more could be said of this famous author, the partisans of that great man, by way of fending off the accusation of atheism, did everything they could to rain hellfire on the head of our philosopher, on this occasion borrowing the tactics of the modern followers of Saint Augustine who, in order to rid themselves of an accusation of Calvinism, have penned the most violent books against that sect. But the persecution which the Cartesians whipped up against Spinoza, and which lasted as long as he lived, only strengthened his resolve in his search for truth.

He thought that most vice was due to imperfect understanding. Therefore, to avoid that hazard, he pushed further into solitude, leaving the place where he was to go to Voorburg, where he reckoned he might find more peace.

The true savants, who missed him immediately, didn't try to deter him at all, and they overwhelmed by their visits just as much in his new village, as they had done in the last one. He was not insensible to the sincere love of good people, and he indulged their insistence that he leave the countryside to live in some city where it would be easier to see him. So, he relocated to The Hague, which he preferred to Amsterdam due to the better quality of its air, and he never moved again.

At first, he was only visited by a small number of friends who only took moderate advantage of his time; but his warm home never lacked for tourists in search of notable landmarks, and the smarter ones of every kind thought they would have wasted a journey had they missed seeing Spinoza.

As his fame spread, every savant wrote letters to him, seeking answers to their own problems. Look how many letters are included in that book that was printed after his death. But, as many visits as he received, so many responses he had made to the savants who wrote him from everywhere, along with his marvelous original books, which are now all our delight, all of this was not enough to keep his genius busy: he spent a few hours every day preparing lenses for microscopes and telescopes, a trade in which he was quite skilled, and if death had not intervened, he may well have revolutionized the study of optics. He was so diligent in the search for truth that, while his health was very poor generally and was always tired, he nevertheless took so little rest that he could spend three whole months indoors. What is more, he refused to a professorship in the academy of Heidelberg, fearing that this sort of career would get in the way of his own plans.

Since he took such pains to correct his understanding, we should not be surprised that his discoveries are without rival. Prior to him, the Holy Scriptures were a hermetic sanctuary—everyone who wrote before him groped about blindly. He alone speaks as a savant in his *Theologico-Political Treatise*; never did one man have such a complete understanding of Jewish antiquity.

Although no wound is more dangerous, nor harder to bear than slander, he was never heard to express his resentment against those who had injured him with it.

Many writers have denounced this book with

bitter insults; but instead of using the same tactics against them, he contented himself with clarifying the parts which they misinterpreted, fearing that their malice might blind some who sought the truth in sincerity. If this book has stirred up a torrent of persecution, it is not the first time that the thoughts of a great man have been misinterpreted, or the first time that a widespread reputation was more dangerous than an evil one.

He was fortunate enough to have known the Grand Pensionary De Witt personally, who had sought to learn mathematics from him, and he often honored him by consulting him on important matters. He had very little care for worldly goods: De Witt left him a pension of two hundred florins when he died, and when his heirs saw the patron's signature to this effect, they tried to get the pension stopped, he put it in their hands without hesitation, as if he had plenty of other sources of income. His disinterested approach led them to reconsider, and they gladly returned to him what they had intended to steal; this was the source of most of his daily bread, since he inherited nothing but a few tangled business affairs from his father, or rather those of the Jews with whom this good man had been doing business, who, judging that Spinoza junior was unable to follow their plotting, embarrassed so profoundly that he chose to abandon everything, rather than to sacrifice his peace for an uncertain hope.

He was so far from seeking public recognition or admiration for his works, that on his deathbed he asked that his name should be omitted from the title page of his book The Ethics, saying that the desire for fame was not worthy of a philosopher. His fame was such that he was spoken of in high circles. The Prince of Condé, who was in Utrecht at the beginning of the last wars, sent him a safe-passage with a letter strongly encouraging him to come and see him.

The mind of Spinoza was too well-made, and he knew only too well what he owed to people of such high rank to fail to heed the request of His Highness. But, never leaving his solitude except to return to it soon after, a journey of several weeks made him uneasy. In the end, after plenty of resistance, his friends persuaded him to be on his way: during this time, an order of the king of France having called the Prince elsewhere, Mr. de Luxembourg received him warmly in his absence, reassuring him of the good intentions of His Highness.

This mob of courtiers didn't bother our philosopher at all. His polite manners were closer to those of the court than to his native, bustling commercial city, whose vices and faults he had escaped.

The prince, who had wanted to see him, often sent for him. The curious people who loved him, and who always found new things to love in him, were joyful to see His Highness oblige him with a visit. After a few weeks, the prince ordered him not to return to Utrecht, and all the curious French were upset by this; for, in spite of the fine offers that Mr. de Luxembourg had offered, our philosopher immediately took his leave of them, and returned to The Hague.

He had a quality, all the more estimable since it is so rare in a philosopher: his extreme neatness; he never left his house except when his clothing displayed that which normally distinguishes an honest man from a pedant.

It is not, he would say, *a messy and sloppy attitude that makes us savants; quite the opposite: this affected sloppiness is the sign of a base soul which lacks all wisdom and where the sciences cannot engender anything but impurity and corruption*. Not only do riches not tempt him, but neither does he fear the unpleasant effects of poverty. His virtue puts him above everything of that sort; and although he was not strong before the good graces of fortune, he never cajoled it, nor murmured against it." If fortune did not always favor him, at any rate his soul was rewarded by being superbly well-stocked with everything that a great man might require. He was liberal in extreme need, lending what little he had from the largesse of his friends with as much generosity as if he had been wealthy himself. Having learned that a man who owed him two hundred florins had gone bankrupt, far from being moved by this said with a smile: "I must cut back my costs to match this small loss. That", he added, "is the price of resolution."

I do not expect the reader to be astounded by this incident; but since his genius is best displayed in these small things, I felt I should include it here.

He was so disinterested that the fanatics who really raised a ruckus against him are few in number. I will add another proof of his disinterestedness, which will show him in no less good a light.

One of his dear friends, a man of means, wanted to present him with two thousand florins, to provide him a more comfortable life, but he refused them with his customary politeness, saying that he had no need for it. In reality, he was so temperate and sober, that he was content with very little. "Nature", he said, "is content with little, and when it is satisfied, so am I." But he was no less equitable than he was disinterested, as will be seen.

The same friend, who had wanted to give him these two thousand florins, having neither wife nor child, wanted to draw up his will in his favor, and to name him as his sole heir. He mentioned it to him, seeking his cooperation and consent. But, far from going along with his friend's plans, Spinoza vigorously told him that it would be against nature if, to the prejudice of one's own brother, he should present his inheritance to a stranger, despite their close friendship. His friend, acquiescing in these wise protestations, left all his goods to their natural beneficiary, on condition that a small annuity of five hundred florins be provided to our philosopher. But the story doesn't end there: he regarded this pension as too large, and had it reduced to three hundred.

What a great example—but I fear it will find few imitators, especially in the Church, greedy as the clergy is for the goods of others, who abuse the infirmity of the elderly, as well as devotees who become infatuated with the church, not only shamelessly accepting any and all inheritances, to the prejudice of their legitimate heirs, but even demanding these as if by right. But let us leave these Tartuffes and return to our philosopher.

Since his health had been poor his whole life long, he had learned to suffer from earliest childhood; this discipline had no better master than Spinoza. He reached for no external consolation; and if he was cognizant of any pain, it was the pain of other people. He said that, "to believe the evil to be lessened by sharing it around, is a sign of ignorance. It is senseless to consider common suffering as a consolation."

This was his state of mind when he shed tears

at the sight of his fellow-citizens ripping their common father to pieces, and although he knew better than anyone what barbarity men are capable of, he didn't shudder at the sight of this fearsome and cruel spectacle. On the one hand, he saw an unprecedented patricide being committed, and an extreme example of ingratitude; on the other he saw himself deprived of an illustrious patron and his sole remaining partisan.

It would have been enough to overwhelm a normal person; but for someone of his caliber, accustomed as he was to mastering all internal turmoil, did not succumb. Since he was always firmly in control of himself, he soon got past these horrific events. One of his friends, who never left his side, mentioned to him how shocking his reaction was. "What wisdom is there", replied our philosopher, "in falling into the mob's passions, and then finding we are too weak to stand up again?"

Since he didn't join any party, he didn't give the prize to any of them: he left to each the liberty of their prejudices; but he maintained that most were an obstacle to truth; that reason was useless if neglected in practice, while its use had been forbidden in all the important choices. "Here", he said, "are the two greatest and most common of human failings: laziness and arrogance. Those who suffer the first failing will stagnate as cowards in crass ignorance, these are no better than animals; others rise as tyrants over the minds of the stupid, giving them a world of illusions and calling it "eternal oracles." That is the source of these absurd beliefs with which men are so infatuated, which divides them one from another, and which is directly opposed to the ends of nature, which is to make them all uniform, as the children of the same mother. This is why he said that "only those who were able to get beyond what they learned as children could ever come to a knowledge of the truth" and that "hard efforts are required to overcome the impressions of tradition and clear out the false ideas which clutter the mind long before it is capable of judging things for itself." To get out of this abyss was, he thought, as great a miracle as that of organizing the chaos.

So, we should not be surprised that he spent his whole life battling superstition; not only was he attracted to the fight by natural inclination, but the teachings of his father, who was a sensible man, also contributed a lot to it. This good man, having taught him to never get it mixed up with solid piety. One time he wanted to test his son, who was then a little under ten years old, he asked him to collect some money from a certain old lady in Amsterdam. When he entered her home and found her reading the Bible, she gave him the sign to wait until she had finished her prayer.

When she had done so, the child told her why he had come; this good old lady counted up the money for him: "Here you go", she said, "pointing to it on her table, this is what I owe your father. May you one day be as honest a man as he is; he has never broken the Law of Moses, and heaven will only bless you to the degree that you act like him." With these words she put the money in the child's sack; but he, remembering that this woman had all the signs of false piety which his father had warned him against, sought to count it as well, in spite of her resistance; when he found two ducatons lacking, which the pious old woman had dropped into a drawer by a slit made for the purpose beneath the table, his suspicions were confirmed. Puffed up with the success of this adventure, and with his father's kudos, he became suspicious of that kind of person, and for a laugh, could imitate them so well that he would surprise all onlookers.

In all his actions, virtue was his object; but since he did not think it as something fearsome, as the Stoics did, he was no enemy of the worthy pleasures. It is true that he made men of intelligence his principal study, and those of the body had few dealings with him. But when he found himself engaged in these sorts of amusements which cannot be dispensed with in good conscience, he regarded them as indifferent, didn't let them disturb his tranquility, which he preferred above all. But what I esteem most in him, is that being born and raised in the midst of a low sort of rabble, which is what spawns superstition, he did not acquire any bitterness, and he purged himself of the false ideas that infatuate most people's minds. He was completely healed from the vapid and ridiculous opinions that the Jews hold about God. A man who knew the end of sound philosophy, and who, endorsed by the most capable people of our age, best put it into practice, such a man, I say, had no interest in thinking that God was as the common people imagined. If he rejected those parts of Moses and the prophets where they are accommodating their teachings to their audience's crude understanding, is that any reason to condemn him? I have read most of the philosophers, and in all honesty, I assure you that not one of them gave the world finer ideas about the Divinity than those which the late Spinoza has given us in his books. He says that the more we know God, the more we master our passions, and in this knowledge, we will come into the perfect acquiescence of our minds and the true love of God, in which our salvation consists, which is blessedness and liberty.

These are the principal points which our philosopher teaches to be reason's dictates regarding the best way of life for, and the highest good of, humanity. If you compare these teachings with the dogmas of the New Testament, you will find them in full harmony. The Law of Jesus Christ brings us to the love of God and our neighbor, which is properly that which reason inspires in us, in Spinoza's view, from which it is easy to see why Saint

Paul calls Christianity a reasonable religion, since reason prescribes it and serves as its basis; a "reasonable religion" being, in Origen's words, all that is subject to the empire of reason. In addition to all of that, an ancient Church Father urged us to live and act according to the rules of reason.

So, these are the rules that our philosopher followed; in this he was supported both by the Church Fathers and the Scriptures. Nevertheless, he was condemned, but only by people whose interest requires that they speak against reason, or by those who have never made its acquaintance.

I have digressed here in order to encourage the simple to shake off the yoke of those envious and the false savants, who, being unable to suffer that good people should enjoy a good reputation, spread lies about them. To return to Spinoza, his conversations displayed an attitude that was so engaging and marked by such correct comparisons, that he unconsciously led everyone else along to share his opinions. He was persuasive, although he did not affect to speak in any polished nor elegant way. He made himself so intelligible, and his discussions were so full of good sense, that nobody heard him who did not go away satisfied.

These fine talents attracted all the great minds of his day, and he always found, in the long run, to keep his composure and make others feel agreeable. Intimacy was always on offer to whoever came to see him; but since the heart of man is always hidden out of sight, and most of these friendships have since been seen to have been contracted with people acting in bad faith, those who were most beholden to him, without any apparent or real reason, ended up treating him with extreme ingratitude.

These false friends, who made a show of adoring him, later did all they could to rip him to shreds, either to please those authorities who care nothing for intellectuals, or to acquire a reputation as a critic.

Once, one of his greatest admirers tried to rile the masses and the magistrates against him; at this he responded blandly: "This is not the first time that the truth comes at great cost. I will not be made to abandon for fear of gossip." Tell me, has greater steadfastness, or a purer virtue ever been seen? Have any of his enemies ever shown so much moderation? But it seems that his misfortune was that he was too good and too enlightened.

He pulled curtains aside which some had tried to keep drawn. He found the Key to the Sanctuary, which was, before him, a mysterious place. Here is why, as good a man as he was, he was always in danger.

Since our philosopher was not one of those austere types who regard marriage as an impediment to the life of the mind, but he did refrain from it himself: either he was afraid of the bad temper of a wife, or because he was entirely devoted to philosophy, and was already in love with the truth.

Aside from the fact that he was not of a very robust complexion, his great application helped also to weaken him; and since late nights are the worst thing for keeping one's health, his discomfort became interminable in company with a progressive fever that he had contracted during his meditations. So that, having been quite poorly during his later years, he finished it early, in mid-course. He lived forty-five years or thereabouts, having been born in 1632, and having ceased to live on the twenty-first of February in 1677.

He was middling in stature; his face was well-proportioned, his skin rather brownish, his hair black and curly, his eyebrows of the same color, with small, black, and lively eyes: he had a rather agreeable, Portuguese, appearance.

With regard to his mind, it was immense and all-penetrating; his demeanor was entirely complacent. He was very good at deflating all ridicule aimed at him, which really made him charming both to the more delicate and the more austere among his friends.

His days were few, but we can say with certainty that he lived an abundant life, having acquired the truly good things in life: that is, virtue; he had nothing further to expect beyond the reputation he had gained by his profound learning. His sobriety, patience and vivacity were the least of his virtues. He was lucky enough to die at the apex of his glory, having soiled it in no way, leaving to the wise and learned behind, regretting this deprivation of his light, which was nearly as useful to them as the rays of the sun. For, although he was not fortunate enough to see his final battles through to the conclusion, in which the States-General regained their empire, albeit in a state of half-loss—either by the bad luck in the fight, or by unfortunate choices—he was in fact quite lucky to thereby escape the storm that his enemies had been preparing for him. They had turned the people against him because he had broken the secret of distinguishing hypocrisy from true piety and of eradicating all superstition.

Our philosopher is therefore quite fortunate, due not only to the splendor of his life, but also by the circumstances of his death, which he endured bravely, as those present have testified; as though he would gladly sacrifice himself, so that the memory of his enemies would not be soiled by his parricide.

But it remains for us to mourn his loss; everyone who has been touched by his writings, and who found that to be in his company was to be strengthened in the path of truth. But, since he was not superior to way of all flesh, let us try to walk in his steps, or, failing that, at least to revere his life with admiration and praise. This is my advice to all strong souls: to follow his teachings and lights, keep them always before your eyes, let them serve as your rule of conduct; that which we love and cherish in great men is always living and will live forever.

Most of those who have lived in obscurity and without glory will remain enshrouded in darkness and forgetfulness; but Baruch de Spinoza will live on in the memory of all true savants and in their writings, which are the temple of immortality.

THE LIFE OF BENEDICT DE SPINOZA

JOHANNES COLERUS

DRAWN FROM THE WRITINGS OF THIS FAMOUS PHILOSOPHER AND THE TESTIMONY OF MANY TRUSTWORTHY PEOPLE WHO KNEW HIM.

1705

Spinoza, the philosopher whose name is so noised about these days, was Jewish in origin. Shortly after his birth, his parents named him Baruch. But, having later abandoned Judaism, he changed his own name, styling himself Benedictus in his books and letters. He was born in Amsterdam on November 24th, 1632. Something that is often said and written about him: namely, that he was poor and of lowly extraction, is not actually true; his parents, Portuguese Jews, respectable and well-off; they were merchants in Amsterdam, they lived in Burgwal, in a rather large house near the old Portuguese synagogue. His manners were, moreover, civil and respectable, and his friends and allies, as well as the goods left by his father and mother show that his origins, as well as his education, were above average. Samuel Carceris, a Portuguese Jew, married the youngest of his two sisters. The elder was called Rebecca, and the younger Miriam de Spinoza, whose son, Daniel Carceris, Benedict de Spinoza's nephew, presented himself as an heir when he died, and got an act passed before the notary Libertus Loef on March 30 1677, in the form of a procuration addressed to Henri Van der Spyck, with whom Spinoza was living at the time of his decease.

HIS FIRST STUDIES.

Spinoza showed from his childhood, and even more so in his youth, that nature had not been unkind to him. That he had a lively imagination and a rapid and perceptive mind is obvious.

Having a great desire to properly learn the Latin tongue, he was first given a tutor from Germany. To perfect his understanding of the language he went to the famous Franciscus van den Enden, who was then in Amsterdam, and also practiced as a doctor of medicine. This man was leading a successful and reputable teaching career, and the wealthier merchants of the city sent him their children—that is, until he was defamed for teaching his pupils something other than Latin; it was eventually revealed that he was sowing the seeds of atheism in the minds of these young people. I could easily prove this fact from the testimony of many respectable people who are still alive, some of whom have been Elders in our church in Amsterdam, and have carried out this function to the edification of all. These good souls always bless the memory of their parents for getting them out of the school of Satan early on: snatching them out of the hands of such a pernicious and impious tutor.

Van den Enden had a single daughter, who knew her Latin, as well as music, so perfectly that she sometimes stood in to teach her father's classes. Spinoza often saw and spoke with her, and he fell in love with her, often saying that he had plans to marry her. She was neither one of the prettiest nor most appealing girl around, but she was intelligent, capable, and cheery, all of which touched Spinoza's heart; but another disciple of Van den Enden, one Kerkering, a native of Hamburg, also had his eyes on her. Aware now that he had a rival, he immediately became jealous; he redoubled his efforts and assiduity towards his mistress. These efforts were carried out to perfection, however, his rival had already given this girl a pearl necklace, to the value of two or three hundred pistoles, which no doubt contributed his winning her good graces. She promised to marry him, and followed through after Mr. Kerkering had left his native Lutheranism for Catholicism. On this story we may consult the Dictionary of Bayle, tome III, edition 2, in the article of Spinoza, on page 2770; as well as Doctor Kortholt's treatise *De Tribus Impostoribus*, in the preface to the second edition.

With regard to Van den Enden, since his case was too well known in Holland to find any work there, he had to look elsewhere. He traveled to France, where he met very unhappy end, after having lived for a few years on his income from his medical practice.

F. Halma, in his Flemish translation of the article on Spinoza, page 5, relates that Van den Enden, having been convicted of the attempted assassination of the Dauphin, was condemned to be hung and executed. However, some who knew him personally in France attest to his execution, but they claim it had a different cause. They say that Van den Enden had tried to foment a rebellion in one of the French provinces, so that the populace might regain their former privileges, which he had his own sights on as well; he thought he might deliver the United Provinces from the oppression they suffered at that time, which gave the French King plenty of trouble in his own country, since he was forced to position a large portion of his forces there; to facilitate the execution of his plans, he had a few ships outfitted, but they arrived too late to be of any use. Whatever the truth, Van den Enden was indeed executed; but if he had tried to assassinate the Dauphin, he had apparently atoned for his crime in another way, and by a much more severe ordeal.

SPINOZA COMES TO THE STUDY OF THEOLOGY, WHICH HE ABANDONS IN FAVOR OF PHYSICS.

After learning Latin very thoroughly, Spinoza turned to the study of theology, and he was dedicated to that for a few years. However, although he already possessed a much intelligence and good judgment, each of these being increased further from one day to the next, and, finding himself drawn more to the study of natural generation and its causes, he abandoned theology to devote himself entirely to physics. He deliberated for a long time about the choice of a tutor, whose writings might serve him for a guide in his studies. Ultimately, the works of Descartes fell into his hands, and he read them avidly; later he often declared it that it was there that he had learned everything he knew about philosophy. He was drawn in by Descartes' declaration that we should never accept anything as true until it has been proven by good, solid arguments. He concluded that the ridiculous principles and doctrines of the Jewish Rabbis could not be accepted by anyone with a good head on their shoulders, since their principles are only based on the authority of the Rabbis themselves, and their doctrine comes not from God, as they claim, but is baseless and lacks the least semblance of rationality.

From then on, he was very reserved in the company of the Jewish Doctors, whom he avoided as much as he could; he was rarely seen in their synagogues, only attending them rarely; this made them extremely angry, for they suspected that he would soon abandon the community and turn Christian. In truth, though, he never did embrace Christianity, nor did he receive the sacred rite of baptism; and although after he abandoned Judaism he did spend a lot of time with some learned Mennonites, and with enlightened members of other Christian denominations, he never joined any of them, and never professed the Faith.

Mr. François Halma, in his book *Het Leven Van Spinoza*, which he had translated into Flemish, reports on pages 6, 7 and 8, that the Jews offered him an annuity shortly after his desertion, hoping to persuade him to stay with them and to attend their synagogues from time to time. This was often confirmed by Spinoza himself to his landlord Mr. Van der Spyck, and to others, adding that the Rabbis had offered to pay him 1,000 florins annually, but that he replied that, were it ten times that amount, he would not have accepted their offer or attended their assemblies for any such reason, since he was no hypocrite and he cared only about seeking the truth. Bayle also reports that he was once attacked by a Jew while leaving the theater, that his face was cut by a knife; and although the wound was not serious, Spinoza thought that the intention had been to kill him. But Spinoza's landlord, as well as his landlord's wife, both of whom are still alive, have recounted this fact to me quite differently. They got it from Spinoza himself, who had told them that one evening, while leaving the old Portuguese synagogue, he saw someone beside him with a dagger in hand; he moved fast and the knife missed its mark, only cutting into his clothes. He kept the *justaucorps* that had been pierced by the blade, to commemorate this event. Since he thought it was no longer safe for him in Amsterdam, he sought to go elsewhere as soon as possible; for he also wanted to pursue his studies and meditations on nature in some peaceful retreat, removed from all the noise of the city.

THE JEWS
EXCOMMUNICATE HIM.

He had no sooner separated from the Jews and their communion than they brought a suit against him, which excommunicated him according to their ecclesiastical laws. He said many times that this is how it happened, and said that from that point on, he severed all ties with them. Bayle agrees with this account, as does Doctor Musæus. Some of the Jews of Amsterdam, who knew Spinoza quite well, have likewise confirmed this fact to me, adding that it was old Chacham Abuabh, at that time a Rabbi of great reputation with them, who publicly pronounced the sentence of excommunication. I have asked the sons of this old Rabbi to share this sentence with me, but in vain; they have protested that they couldn't find it among their father's papers; but it was obvious that they had no real desire to part with it, or to share it with anyone.

One day here in The Hague, I happened to ask a learned Jew what was the formula that is used to ban or excommunicate an apostate. I was told that it could be found in the writings of Maimonides, Treatise *Hilcoth Talmud Torah*, chapter 7, v. 2, and that it was not very long.

However, all the interpreters of Scripture think that there were three kinds of excommunication among the ancient Jews;

although this view is not followed by the learned Johannis Seldeni, who only mentions two in his treatise *De Synedriis Et Praefecturis Juridicis Veterum Ebraeorum*, Book 1, chapter 7, page 64. They call the first kind of excommunication the *Niddui*, which has two parts: first, the guilty is separated and enclosed in the entryway of the synagogue for one week, after severely reprimanding and firmly exhorting him to repent and seek forgiveness for his fault. If he fails to do this, he is given thirty more days or a month to think about his actions.

During that time, he was forbidden to come within eight or ten paces of anyone, and nobody dared any longer to have any dealings with him, except those who brought him food and drink; and this ban was called the "minor" excommunication. Hoffmann, in his *Lexicon*, Vol II, page 213, adds that it was completely forbidden to drink and eat with such a man or to use the same bath as him; that he could still attend their assemblies if he so wished, but only to listen and take instruction. But if, during this term of a month, a son was born to him, circumcision was to be refused to the child; and if it happened to die, nobody was allowed to cry about it or show any sign of mourning; on the contrary, to heap eternal infamy on this cursed child, they would cover its grave with a mound of stones or roll a single large stone to cover the place entirely.

Mr. Goerée, in his book *Antiquités judaïques*,

volume I, page 641, maintains that among the Hebrews nobody was ever punished by a particular ban or excommunication, and nothing like it was in use; but virtually all of the interpreters of Holy Scripture say the opposite, and there are few, either Jew or Christian, who agree with him.

The second kind of ban or excommunication was called *Cherem*. This is banishment from the synagogue accompanied by horrible curses, which mostly come from the book of Deuteronomy, chapter 28, this is according to Doctor Dilherr, who discussed this at length in volume II, p. 319 of his *Disputatio Philologica*. The learned Lightfoot, while discussing I Corinthians, 5:5, in volume II p. 89 of his *Works*, teaches that this interdiction or banishment was also used when the term of thirty days had passed and the accused refused to recognize his guilt; then, according to his view, the second part of the minor ban or excommunication went into effect. Several curses from the Law of Moses were then solemnly pronounced against the guilty in presence of the whole community, in a public assembly. Candles or chandelles were then lit; these burned down while the sentence of excommunication was read aloud; which having been completed, the Rabbi extinguished them as a sign that this unhappy man had been abandoned to his reprobate ways and entirely deprived of the divine light. After one of these bans, the accused was no longer allowed to attend their assemblies, even as an earnest seeker. However, he was given a further delay of one month, which could be extended to two or three, in hopes that they would reconsider their ways and ask forgiveness for their sin; but when this also failed, they finally fulminated the third and final excommunication.

It was this third kind of excommunication that they called *Schammatha*. This was a ban, or banishment, from their assemblies or synagogues, which forbade them from entering them ever again; this was called their Great Anathema, or banishment. When the Rabbis published it in the assembly, they had, from the earliest times, a custom of blowing the horn, in order to terrify the minds of the attendees all the more. By this excommunication, the criminal was deprived of the aid and assistance from anyone, as well as the succor and grace and mercy of God, abandoned to his most severe judgments, and handed forever over to an inevitable ruin and condemnation. Many think this excommunication the same thing mentioned in I Corinthians 16:22, where the apostle calls it *Maranatha*. Here is the passage: "If there is anyone who does not love the Lord Jesus, let him be anathema *maharam motha* or *maranatha*;" that is to say, let him be anathema or excommunicated forever; or, as others would have it, "the Lord comes", that is, to judge this excommunicant and punish him. The Jews teach that blessed Enoch is the author of this excommunication, that they got it from him, and that it has been handed down to them by a certain and incontestable tradition.

With regard to the reasons why someone might be excommunicated, the Jewish Doctors give two principal ones, according to Lightfoot as cited above: namely, either negligence in one's debts or because of a libertine or Epicurean lifestyle.

Debts could also be punished by excommunication when the debtor had been ordered to pay up, and refused to make things right with his creditors. This was also the penalty for following a licentious and Epicurean way of life; it was also used against a person convicted of blasphemy, idolatry, breaking the Sabbath, or deserting religion and one's duty to God. In the *Talmud Sanhedrin*, folio 99, an Epicurean is defined as someone who holds the word of God in disregard and ridicules the teaching of the sages, and whose tongue speaks evil against the divine majesty.

To such men they granted no stay. They incurred immediate excommunication. First they were named and cited on the first day of the week by the doorman of the synagogue; and, as he normally refused to present himself to them, he who had cited him then publicly announces these words: "I have, by order of the director of the School, cited so and so, who has failed to respond to the citation, and has not presented himself to us." Then they proceeded to the sentence of excommunication, and their target was from then on designated an outlaw and was served with an act of interdiction or banishment, a copy of which was made available to anyone, for a fee. On the other hand, if he did present himself and maintained his opinions, his excommunication was only pronounced orally; to which the assistants added a further insult of trampling on him and otherwise ridiculing him.

Besides these two causes for excommunication, the learned Lightfoot, mentioned above, lists twenty-four others he has discovered in the writings of the ancient Jews; but that would take us too far afield, and his discussion of the matter is too extensive to be included here.

Ultimately, as for the formula used in the sentences of excommunication declared orally or expressed in writing, here is what Doctor Seldeni says, in the place cited above, on p. 59, which he found in one of Maimonides's books: "First the accusation, or the cause of the proceedings, was pronounced; and the following brief formula of the curses was then added: "So and so is excommunicated by the excommunication *Niddui/Cherem/Schammatha*. May he be separated, banished, or entirely extirpated from among us."

I have long searched for the wording of any of the formulas which the Jews used in these excommunications, but in vain; no Jew has either been able or willing to share any of them with me. But in the end, the learned Mr. Surenbusius, a professor of Eastern languages in the "Illustrious School" of Amsterdam, who has a perfect knowledge of Jewish customs and writings, has put into my hands the formula of the normal and general excommunication which was used to extirpate from their numbers all those who lived badly or disobeyed the Law. It is taken from the Jewish ceremony called *Kolbo*, and he has given it to me in Latin translation. We may, however, read it in Seldeni, p. 524, in book 4, chapter 7 of his treatise *De Jure Naturæ et Gentium*.

Spinoza, having been separated completely from the Jewish community—whose Doctors he had irritated by contradicting them and uncovering their absurd deceptions—therefore we should not be surprised to see him accused of blasphemy, of being an enemy of God's Law, and an apostate. He had no sooner withdrawn from them than he threw himself into the arms of infidels; and we must not doubt that they fulminated the harshest of excommunications against him. This has been confirmed for me by a learned Jew, who also assured me that if Spinoza was excommunicated, then it would have been the anathema *Schammatha* that was used in his case. But since Spinoza was absent at this ceremony, the sentence of excommunication was passed in writing, and a copy of it was then served to him. He appealed his excommunication, writing a response to it, in Spanish, to the Rabbis; they responded to this document in a way that will be shown later.

SPINOZA LEARNS A TRADE, OR A MECHANICAL ART.

The Law of the ancient Jewish Doctors plainly states that it is not enough to be educated, but that one should also practice some mechanical art or profession, to be ready for any eventuality, and to make a living. This is positively stated by Rabbi Gamaliel in Talmud *Pirke Avoth*, chapter 2. He teaches that the study of the Law is something very desirable when combined with a profession or some mechanical art; for, he says, the continual application to these two exercises leaves no time or attention for evil deeds; and every educated man who fails to learn some kind of trade will end up disordered and loose in their morals; Rabbi Yehuda adds that if any man fails to teach his children a trade, he might as well teach them to be brigands.

Spinoza, educated in the Law and customs of the ancients, was aware of this instruction and kept it in mind, even though he was now both separated and excommunicated from the Jewish community. He took advantage of such wise and reasonable advice, and learned a mechanical art prior to establishing himself in the tranquil and retired life he yearned for. Thus, he learned to make lenses for binoculars and other uses, and he became so skilled in s were widely sought after, and this brought him a decent livelihood. After his death, a great many polished lenses were found in his cabinet; these were sold at high price by the public vendor who attended the inventory of these and the rest of his belongings.

Having mastered this art, he then taught himself to draw, and became very expert in producing portraits in ink or charcoal. I hold in my hands a complete book of his portraits, which contains the likenesses of many distinguished people who he knew or who paid a visit to him. In the fourth leaf of this book a fisherman is portrayed in his shirt, with a net on his right shoulder, very like the pose of Masaniello, the famous Neapolitan rebel leader, as he is depicted in history, in intaglio. While mentioning this drawing, I should not omit that Mr. Van der Spyck, with whom Spinoza was a lodger at the time of his death, has assured me that this pencil or portrait resembled Spinoza very well, and that it was assuredly he himself who was depicted. It is not necessary to mention all the distinguished people whose portraits are also in this book, among his other drawings.

In this way he was able to earn a living with his hands and devote himself to his studies, as he had resolved to do. Therefore, since nothing was keeping him in Amsterdam, he moved in with an acquaintance who lived on the road that leads from Amsterdam to

Auwerkerke. There he spent his time studying and working on his lenses; when they were polished, his friends took care of collecting them from him, having them sold, and having the money sent to him.

HE GOES TO LIVE IN RIJNSBURG, FOLLOWED BY VOORBURG, AND FINALLY IN THE HAGUE.

In the year 1664 Spinoza left this place and retired to Rijnsburg, near Leiden, where he spent the winter; but soon after this he departed for Voorburg, near The Hague, as he says in his thirtieth letter, written to Pierre Balling. I have been informed that he spent three or four years there. During this time, he became friendly with a great many people in The Hague, all of whom were of distinguished rank or high office in either government or the military. They gladly spent time in his company, loving to hear what he had to say. It was at their insistence that he finally took up residence in The Hague, where he lived first in a boarding house on the Veerkade with the Van Velden widow, in the same house where I am currently a tenant. My study, on the second floor at the back of the house, is the same room where he would sleep, study, and work. He often had food brought here, and two or three days would pass without anyone seeing him. But, finding the rent a little too high, he leased a back room on the Paviljoensgracht from Mr. Henri Van der Spyck, to whom I will often refer. He arranged to have food and drink brought to him, and he lived at his leisure, in a very reclusive manner.

HE WAS VERY SOBER AND VERY FRUGAL.

It is almost incredible how sober and domestic he was all this time. It wasn't that he was reduced to such a great state of poverty, that he couldn't have spent more had he so desired, since so many people offered him their purse and every kind of assistance; but he was naturally sober and content with little, and he recoiled at the idea of being seen to live, even for a moment, at someone else's expense. His utter sobriety and thrift is also proven by various small accounting books that were among the papers he left behind. Here we find that all he ate one day was one soup with milk, seasoned with butter, which cost three *sous*, and a pot of beer at one and a half *sou*; on another day he ate nothing but gruel with raisins and butter: this plate cost him four and a half *sous*. In these same accounts one finds him paying for no more than two half-pints of wine, at most, in any month; and although he was often invited to dinner, he preferred to live from his own fare, however meager this was, rather than feast at the expense of another.

This is how he spent the rest of his life with his final landlord, for a little over five and a half years. He was very careful to adjust his accounts each quarter, to avoid going over-budget for the year. He would sometimes tell those of the household that he was like a serpent forming a circle with its tail in its mouth, to illustrate that he never had a surplus in any year. He added that it was not his idea to amass anything beyond what it would cost to be buried with decorum, and that, since his parents hadn't left him anything, his own kin and heirs had little to expect by way of an inheritance.

HIS PERSON AND HIS MANNER OF DRESS.

Regarding his person, his height and facial features, there are still lots of people in The Hague who would have seen and known him personally. He was of medium height; his facial features were well proportioned, his skin somewhat dark, his hair curly and black, while his eyebrows long and of the same color, so that at a glance he was immediately recognizable as a descendant of Portuguese Jews. As to his clothing, he was quite unconcerned about it, and his garments were generally no better than those of the simplest bourgeois male. A very important Counselor of the State, having stopped by to see him, found him in a dressing-gown that was quite unsuited to the occasion: the Counselor reprimanded him somewhat and offered him another one; Spinoza responded that a man would not be improved for having a nicer robe. It is against common sense, he added, to put a cheap article in an expensive bag.

HIS MANNERISMS, HIS CONVERSATION, AND HIS DISINTERESTEDNESS.

Moreover, if his lifestyle was very seemly, his conversation was no less gentle and peaceable. He was quite aware of his own mastery of his passions. He was never seen to be either very sad or very excited. He knew how to control his anger, and when misfortunes came his way, he never let himself be seen to be out of control; at most, if he needed to show his anger by some gesture or by certain words, he never failed to retire immediately so that he would do nothing unseemly. He was also extremely affable and had an easy manner, often speaking to his landlady, particularly when he was going to bed, and to those of the house, when some affliction or malady had come upon them; he did not fail, at such times, to console them and exhort them to patiently suffer the evils that God had destined for them. He advised children to go to church often, as well as saying that they should obey and submit to their parents' will. When the people of the lodging returned from the sermon, he often asked them what they had gained from it; what they had remembered for their edification. He had a great esteem for my predecessor, Doctor Cordes, who was a learned man, who displayed a good temperament and led an exemplary life; Spinoza often sang his praises. He even sometimes went to hear his preaching, and above all noted his learned manner of expounding the Scriptures and the sound life-applications he offered. He suggested that his landlord and those of the household should never miss any of the sermons of such a capable man.

One day his landlady asked him whether she could be saved in her religion; this is what he said in reply: "Your religion is good, and you should not seek another one, nor should you doubt that you will get salvation in it, as long as you devote yourself to piety and lead a peaceable and tranquil life."

While he remained in the lodging, he inconvenienced no-one, and he spent most of his time quietly in his room. When he wanted to get away from his philosophical meditations, he would go downstairs to unwind, and have normal, even trifling conversations with those of the household. Sometimes he would amuse himself by smoking a tobacco pipe; and when he wanted to have a little fun, he would collect some spiders and make them fight, or he would throw flies in the spider's webs, enjoying the ensuing battle so gleefully that he sometimes burst out laughing. He also used a microscope to examine the body parts of the smallest insects, which led him to the conclusions that best seemed suit his discoveries.

Moreover, he had no interest in money, as I have mentioned, and he was quite content if he had enough to for his food and shelter each day. Simon de Vries, of Amsterdam, who shows a great deal of affection for him in the twenty-sixth letter, calling him his faithful friend (*amice integerrime*), once offered him a gift of 2,000 florins, to let him live a little more comfortably; but Spinoza, in the presence of his landlord, gracefully declined the money, on pretext that he didn't need anything, and that if he accepted so much money, it would certainly interfere with his studies and his meditations.

When the same Simon de Vries was at death's door, who had neither wife nor children, he wanted to make out his will and institute Spinoza as his sole heir; but Spinoza did not consent, insisting that his friend should not dream of leaving his goods to anyone but his closest relative and natural heir, i.e., his brother who was living in Schiedam.

This was carried out as he had advised; however, it was on condition that Simon de Vries's brother and heir had to give Spinoza a lifelong pension to cover his living costs; this clause was faithfully executed. But note how peculiarly Spinoza behaved: he was offered a pension of 500 florins, which he said was too much. It was reduced to 300 and was given in regular intervals to him for the rest of his life; even after he died, Mr. De Vries of Schiedam was careful to settle accounts with his landlord Mr. Van der Spyck; this is confirmed in a letter of Jean Rieuwertz (a printer in Amsterdam) who was tasked to carry it out. The letter is dated March 6, 1678 and is addressed to Van der Spyck himself.

We can also see Spinoza's disinterestedness in the incident that occurred after his father died; the inheritance was to be divided between his sisters and himself. They had sought to exclude him entirely, and he brought a successful lawsuit against them. However, when the time came to collect the goods, he just left it all to them, only carrying off a small bed for himself, which was actually quite a good one, along with its valance.

HE IS KNOWN BY MANY
VERY IMPORTANT PEOPLE.

Spinoza had no sooner published a few of his books than his reputation was made among the most distinguished of all people, who considered him a rare genius and a great philosopher. Mr. Stoupe, lieutenant-colonel in a Swiss regiment serving the French monarch, was stationed at Utrecht in 1673. He had been previously a minister in the Savoy in London, during the troubles in England, and in the days of Cromwell; he was then made a brigadier, and by carrying out the functions of this charge he was killed in the battle of Steenkerque. While he was in Utrecht he wrote a book entitled *De Gods-dienst der Hollanders*, where he criticizes, among other things, the Reformed theologians for allowing the publication, in 1670, and on their watch, the book that bears the title of the *Theologico-Political Treatise*, of which Spinoza declares himself the author in his nineteenth letter. However, Stoupe takes no trouble to refute or respond to this book. But the celebrated professor Braunius, of the university of Groningen, has shown the opposite to be true in his refutation of Mr. Stoupe's book; and in reality, so many things were published against this abominable *Treatise* that Mr. Stoupe is clearly mistaken. In those days he had been corresponding quite frequently with Spinoza, and he ultimately begged Spinoza to come to Utrecht at a certain time. Mr. Stoupe wanted to attract him there all the more since the prince of Condé, who had then seized control of the government of Utrecht, had eagerly sought a meeting with Spinoza; and this is why it was assured that His Highness was so eager to do him a favor with respect to the king, as he had hopes of easily obtaining a pension for Spinoza, provided only that he would dedicate one of his books to His Majesty. He received this dispatch, with a passport enclosed, and departed soon after receiving it. Mr. Halma, in his *Life* of our philosopher, which he translated and excerpted from Mr. Bayle's *Dictionnaire*, reports on page 11 that he is certain that he did actually visit the prince of Condé, holding various meetings with him on several days, along with many other distinguished individuals, and with the lieutenant-colonel Stoupe. But Van der Spyck and his wife, with whom he had lodged and who are still living, have assured me that, upon his return, he positively told them that he had not been able to see the prince of Condé, who had departed from Utrecht a few days before he arrived. Rather, in his conversations with Mr. Stoupe, the latter had assured him that he would do everything he could for him, and that his recommendation would secure him the king's liberality in the form of a pension. However, Spinoza had no plans to dedicate any book whatsoever to the French monarch, and he had declined this offer as gracefully as he could.

After his return, the populace of The Hague was extraordinarily upset about him; he had been branded as a spy, and it was suggested that a dangerous man like him had best be on his way, since he had dealt so openly with the enemy. Spinoza's landlord was alarmed at the goings-on, understandably afraid that the mob might drag him out of his house after having forced the door down and perhaps looting his home; but Spinoza reassured him and consoled him as best he could, saying:

> Don't worry about my welfare; I am safe: many notable men of the country know quite well the reasons why I undertook the journey. But, whatever happens, upon the least noise at your door I will walk straight out to them, even if they want to do the same with me as with the poor gentlemen De Witt. I am a good republican and have never had any aims but the glory and advantage of my State.

In the same year the Elector Palatine Charles-Louis, of glorious memory, got wind of this great philosopher's capacity, and wanted to lure him to Heidelberg as a professor of philosophy; no doubt this was in complete ignorance of the venom that was at that time still hidden in Spinoza's bosom, and which in later times would be more openly expressed. His Electoral Highness gave the order to the famous Doctor Fabricius, a good philosopher and one of his advisers, to deliver this proposal to Spinoza. He extended the offer, in the name of his prince, of a chair in philosophy, along with wide latitude in reasoning according to his principles as he thought best, *cum amplissima philosophandi libertate*. But this offer came with a condition which did not suit Spinoza at all: for, whatever freedom would be granted to him, he must never use it to undermine the established religion. For further information see Doctor Fabricius's letter, written at Heidelberg, and dated on the 16th of February (see *Opera Posthuma*, letter 53, page 561). Here the reader will see that Spinoza his regaled with the title of "very famous philosopher of a transcendent genius": *philosopher acutissime ac celeberrime*.

This was a pit that he was quick to jump over, if I may be allowed such an expression; he saw the difficulty, or rather the impossibility of reasoning according to his principles, while at the same time teaching nothing contrary to the established religion. He wrote his response to Mr. Fabricius on March 30, 1673, very politely refusing the offered chair of philosophy. He said that "the duty of teaching the young would get in the way of his own studies", and he "was never minded to embrace such a profession." But that was only a pretext, which is plain enough in the words that follow: "Moreover, I must note", he said to the Doctor, "that you I cannot set any bounds to my liberty of expression, even to spare the feelings of religion, *Cogito deinde me nescire quibus limitibus libertas illa philosophandi intercludi debeat, ne videar publice stabilitam religionem perturbare velle*" (See his *Opera Posthuma*, p. 563, Letter 54).

HIS WRITINGS AND HIS OPINIONS.

With regard to his works, some of what has been attributed to him may not have come from his pen; some have been lost, or at least are not publicly available; others have been printed and given to the world.

Mr. Bayle stated that Spinoza wrote a defense of his leaving the Synagogue in Spanish, but this was never printed. He also said that large portions of that defense were later reused in the *Theologico-Political Treatise*; but I have been unable to learn anything about this defense, despite having requested a copy from those who knew him well, and who are yet very much alive.

In 1664 he sent his book to the printers, called *Renati Descartes Principiorum philosophiæ pars prima et secunda more geometrico demonstratæ* ("Principles of the Philosophy of Descartes Demonstrated Geometrically, First and Second Parts"), which was soon followed by his *Metaphysical Meditations* (Cogitata metaphysica). Had he stopped there, this unfortunate man would have retained a well-earned reputation as a wise and enlightened philosopher.

However, in 1665, a little book, in duodecimo, appeared bearing the title of *On the Rights of*

Ecclesiastics, by Lucius Antistius Constans, printed in Alethopolis, with Caius Valerius Pennatus[2]. The author strives to prove that the spiritual and political rights which the clergy claims, and which others claim for it, are not rightfully given to it, and that the clergy abuse it scandalously, and that all of their authority depends entirely on that of the magistrates or rulers, who hold the place of God in the cities and republics where the clergy is established; and thus the pastors should never meddle with and promulgate their own religions, but should teach whatever the magistrates want. Note that all of that is based in the same ideas that Hobbes taught in *Leviathan.*

Bayle informs us that the style, the Principles and organization Antistius's book are very close to those of Spinoza in his book, the *Theologico-Political Treatise*; but this does not really prove anything. The fact that this *Treatise* appeared exactly at the same time when Spinoza began to write his own, and that the *Theologico-Political Treatise* came out shortly afterwards, is no proof that one was in any way related to the other. It is quite easy for two people to write and teach the same impieties at the same time; and because their writings did appear at about the same time, there is no reason to conclude that they came from the same pen. Spinoza himself, when

---

[2] Lucii Antistii Constantis de jure Ecclesiasticorum, Alethopoli, apud Cajum Valerium Pennatum.

asked by a person of great importance whether he wrote the first *Treatise*, positively denied it, which I have had confirmed by trustworthy witnesses. The use of Latin in these books, and their style and ways of speaking are not as close as has been claimed: the first shows a profound respect when speaking of God; he often calls God "very good" and "very great", *Deum ter optimum maximum*. But I find no parallel expressions anywhere in Spinoza's writings.

Many learned people have assured me that this impious book entitled The Holy Scriptures Explained by Philosophy, *Philosophia sacræ Scripturæ interpres*, and the Treatise which we have discussed came from the same author, that is, L... M... And although it seems very probable to me, I leave it to the judgment of those who might have more specific knowledge of the matter.

Spinoza published his *Theologico-Political Treatise* in 1670. Its Flemish translator thought it suitable to title it *De Regtzinnige Theologant, of Godgeleerde Staattkunde*; i.e., The Judicious Politician and Theologian. Spinoza confirms his authorship plainly in his nineteenth letter, addressed to Henry Oldenburg; in the same letter he asks his friend to write back with any objections that knowledgeable people might have to his book; he had thought to publish a revised second edition. On the bottom of the title page, we can fortunately see that it was printed in

Hamburg, by Henri Conrad. However, we can rest assured the magistrate and the venerable ministers of Hamburg would never have allowed so much impiety to be published and disseminated in their city.

Rather, the book was doubtlessly printed in Amsterdam, by Christophe Conrad, on the Egelantiersgracht. In 1679, having been called to that city on certain business, Conrad himself brought made a gift to me of me several copies of this *Treatise*, being himself unaware of how pernicious this book was.

The Dutch translator also thought it appropriate to honor the city of Bremen with such a worthy production, as if his translation had issued from the press of Hans Jurgen Van der Weyl in 1694. But what is said of these editions of Bremen and Hamburg is false, and the same kind of obstacles would have prevented the book being published in either of these cities. Philopater, whom we have already mentioned, says openly in the *Sequel* to his Life, on page 231, that the old man Jean Hendrikzen Glasemaker, whom I knew quite well, had translated this work; and he assures us at the same time that he had also translated Spinoza's *Opera Posthuma* into Dutch, in 1677. Moreover, he paid such close attention to Spinoza's *Treatise* and praised it so highly that nobody ever rivaled him. The author, or at least the printer of the *Sequel* to the *Life of Philopater*, that is, Aard Wolsgryck, formerly a bookseller in Amsterdam, on the corner of the Rosmarijnsteeg, was duly punished for this insolence, and confined in the house of correction, to which he was sentenced for a few years. I ask with all my heart God may touch his heart during his time there, and that he may reform his views when he leaves. This is the state of mind I hope he was in when I saw him here in The Hague last summer, where he had come to ask the booksellers for remuneration for some books he had previously printed and delivered to them.

To return to Spinoza and his *Theologico-Political Treatise*, I will say what I think, but I will first relate the judgment of two well-known writers, the first of whom follows the Confession of Augsburg and the other is Reformed. The first is Spitzelius, who speaks this way in his Treatise which is entitled *Infelix literator*, on page 363:

> This impious author (Spinoza), by a prodigious presumption that blinded him, has pushed the limits of impudence and impiety by maintaining that the prophecies are not based in anything but the imagination of the prophets, that they were subject to error, as were also the Apostles, and that both had written naturally, and according to their own understanding, without any revelation or command from God; that they had, moreover, accommodated religion as far as possible to the capacity of those living at the time, and based it on principles that were known and

accepted in their day.

Irreligiosissimus auctor, stupenda sui
fidentia plane fascinatus, eo progressus
impudentiæ et impietatis fuit, ut prophetiam
dependisse dixerit a fallaci imaginatione
prophetarum, eosque pariter ac apostolos
non ex revelatione et divino mandato
scripsisse, sed tantum ex ipsorummet
naturali judicio; accommodavisse insuper
religionem, quoad fieri potuerit, hominum
sui temporis ingenio, illamque fundamentis
tum temporis maxime notis et acceptis
superædificasse.

This is the very method that Spinoza, in his
Theologico-Political Treatise, claims that we
can and should use, even now, in interpreting
the Holy Scriptures; for he maintains, among
other things, that "just as the Scriptures were
originally produced in conformity with the
established opinions and within the reach of
the masses, in the same way it is given to
each to interpret them according to their own
understanding; and to adjust them in line with
their own opinions."

If that were true, good God! Where would we
all be? How could we say that the Scriptures
are divinely inspired, that the prophecies are
reliable, that the saints who wrote them spoke
and wrote by God's command and the
inspiration of the Holy Spirit, when the
Scriptures are quite certainly true, as a sure
testimony of their truth is confirmed to our
consciences, and that they are the ultimate

judge whose rulings are the sure and unshakable rule of our beliefs, our thoughts, our faith and our very life? If we grant the opposite, we might well say that the Holy Bible is just a ball of wax that we can bend and shape as we please, or a kaleidoscope in which everyone sees whatever strikes their fancy, a true *bonnet de fou* that can be adjusted and turned at will a hundred different ways. The Lord confound you, Satan, and shut your mouth!

Spitzelius was not content merely to say what he thought about this pernicious book; he also adduced the views of Mr. Manseveld, formerly a professor at Utrecht. In a book printed in 1674 in Amsterdam, he wrote as follows: "We esteem that this *Treatise* must be forever buried in the darkness of the deepest forgetfulness" *Tractatum hunc ad æternas damnamdum tenebras*, etc." All of which is quite apt, since this unfortunate *Treatise* subverts Christianity from top to bottom, sapping all the authority of the Sacred Writings, upon which it is uniquely based and established.

The second witness I will produce is Mr. Guillaume Van Blyenburg, of Dordrecht, who maintained a long correspondence with Spinoza, and who, in his thirty-first one, found in the *Opera Posthuma* on page 476, says that he himself "embraced no party nor vocation, and that he only lives by the honest business he conducts" (*Liber sum, nulli adstrictus professioni; honestis mercaturis me alo*). This merchant, a well-educated man, in the preface to a work called, *La Vérité de la Religion Chrétienne*, printed in 1674 at Leiden, expresses his estimation of Spinoza's *Treatise*:

> This book is filled with curious, but abominable discoveries, the learning and research of which can only have originated in the infernal regions. Neither any Christian nor any intelligent man should regard this sort of book with anything but horror. Its author tries to ruin the Christian religion and all our hopes that depend thereon; in their place he introduces atheism, or at best a natural religion forged according to the whim or interest of the rulers. In this new religion, evil would only be suppressed by fear of punishment; and when neither execution nor justice is feared, a man without a conscience may do anything he likes...

I will now add that I have carefully read Spinoza's book from cover to cover; and I declare before God that I found nothing there that is the least bit threatening or destructive to my faith in the Gospel truths. Instead of solid proofs, it contains little more than suppositions and what are called, in academic circles, *petitiones principii*. And once you deny and reject his so-called proofs, nothing remains of his book but lies and blasphemy. Since he offers neither arguments nor proofs for his claims, does he think we should believe him blindly, taking him at his mere word?

Finally, various writings that Spinoza left after his death were printed in 1677, which was also the year he died. These are what are called his *Posthumous Works*, or *Opera Posthuma*. The three capital letters B. D. S. were printed on the head of the title page, and the book contains five treatises: the first is a treatise on ethics, demonstrated geometrically (*Ethica more geometrico demonstrata*); the second is a work on politics; the third is a treatise on the understanding and the means of improving it (*De emendatione intellectus*); the fourth volume is a collection of letters and responses (*Epistolæ et responsiones*); the fifth, a short Hebrew Grammar (*Compendium grammatices linguæ hebreæ*). Neither the printer's name is given nor is its place of publication; which indicates that its publisher wanted to remain anonymous. However, Spinoza's landlord, Mr. Henri Van der Spyck, who still has many years of life ahead of him, told me that Spinoza had requested that immediately after his death, the desk in which he stored his letters and papers should be sent to Jean Rieuwertz, a printer in Amsterdam; Van der Spyck faithfully carried out this request according to Spinoza's will. And Jean Rieuwertz, by his response to Mr. Van der Spyck, dated March 25, 1677 in Amsterdam, confirmed having received the aforementioned desk. He adds on the end of his letter that

Spinoza's family would like to know to

whom it had been sent, because they had it in their heads that it had been packed full of money, and they told this to the boatmen involved in shipping it; but, he said, if the register of water-borne parcels is not on file in The Hague, I can't imagine how they might have known anything about this desk, and it's actually better if they never find anything out about it...

And he finished his letter thus, which clearly shows who was responsible for letting such an abominable book see the light of day.

Enough learned people have exposed the impieties contained in these *Posthumous Works*, and have warned everyone to be on guard against them. I can only little to what they have already written. His treatise on Ethics begins by definitions or descriptions of the Divinity. Who would doubt that, starting like that, that this must be the work of some Christian philosopher? All the definitions are magnificent, in particular the sixth one, where Spinoza says that "God is an infinite being, that is, a substance containing an infinity of attributes, each of which represents and expresses an eternal and infinite essence." But when we examine these views in detail, we find that Spinoza's God is but a phantom, an imaginary God, which is anything but God. Thus, to this philosopher we may well apply the words of the Apostle regarding impious in Titus 1:16: "They profess to recognize a God by their words, but in their works they deny

Him." What David says of the impious in Psalm 14:1 also suits him very well: "The fool says in his heart that there is no God." Whatever Spinoza says, this it really what he thinks. He takes the liberty of using the word God, but uses it in a sense opposite to everything that Christians have ever understood by it. He himself says as much in his twenty-first letter, to Mr. Oldenburg: "I recognize", he says," that I have a very different idea of God than what the modern Christians make of him." and "I regard God as the principle and cause of all things, immanent and not passing (*Deum, rerum omnium causam immanentem, non vero transeuntem, statuo*)." And to support his views, he uses the words of Saint Paul in Acts 17:28, which he bends to his own meaning: "In God we have our life, our movement and our being."

To understand his opinion, we must consider that a passing cause is one whose productions are external to, and outside of, itself, like someone who tosses a stone in the air or a carpenter who builds a house, instead of an immanent cause acting internally, without requiring any input from the outside. Thus, when our soul thinks or desires something, it halts in this thought or desire without going outside itself, and it is constituted as its own immanent cause. In the same way, Spinoza's God is the cause of this universe, and God is not placed somewhere beyond it. But since we know that the universe has boundaries, this would imply that God is a limited and finite being. And although he says that God is infinite and contains an infinity of attributes in Himself, he has to distort the terms *eternal* and *infinite*, since by them he cannot refer to a being which has existed of itself before all time and before any other being had been created; but he calls everything to which human understanding cannot find an end or a boundary, infinite; for the productions of God, according to him, are so numerous that man, even with all his power and intelligence, cannot grasp them. In addition, they are so well supported, so solid, and so well integrated that they will last forever.

Nevertheless, he assures us in his twenty-first letter that those people are wrong who impute to him the idea that God and matter, where God acts, are but one and the same thing. But he must agree that matter is something essential to the Divinity who exists alone and who only acts within the world of matter, that is to say, within the universe. The God of Spinoza is thus nothing other than nature itself, infinite to be sure, but also corporeal and material, taken in general and with all its modifications. For he assumes that there are two eternal properties in God: *cogitatio* and *extensio*, that is, thought and extension. By the first of these properties God is contained within the universe; by the second, God is the universe itself: in combination, this pair constitute what we call God.

As far as I have been able to understand

Spinoza's views, this is the pivot point of the dispute between him and us Christians, to wit: if the true God is an eternal substance, different and distinct from the universe and all of nature; and if, by an act of entirely free will, He has drawn the world and all creatures from non-existence, or if the universe and all beings that it contains constitute an essential part of the nature of God, considering the latter as a substance whose thoughts and extension are infinite. This last proposition is what Spinoza believes: see *Anti-Spinoza* by Wittichius, p. 18 and onwards. Therefore, he certainly does affirm God as the general cause of all things, but he claims that God produced them by necessity, without exercising any liberty in this act: without choosing to do it or having any inclination. Everything that happens in the world, either good or evil, virtue or crime, sin or good works, necessarily comes from Him; and by consequence He must not incline Himself, either to judgment or punishment, resurrection salvation, or damnation; for otherwise this imaginary God would only be punishing and rewarding the workmanship of His own hands, as a child might do with a doll. Is this not the most pernicious form of atheism ever to appear in the world? This is what leads Mr. Burmannus, a Reformed preacher in Enkhuizen, to rightly name Spinoza as the most impious atheist who ever lived.

I do not intend to analyze each of Spinoza's impieties and absurdities; I have shared a few only, keeping to the most salient ones, with hopes of averting the Christian reader to regard such a pernicious doctrine with aversion and horror. However, I must not omit that, in second part of his *Ethics*, p. 40, he states plainly that the soul and body are one and the same being, whose properties are, as he puts it, thought and extension: "When I speak of the body, I mean nothing other than a modality that expresses the essence of God in a certain and precise manner, considered as an extended thing (*Per corpus intelligo modum qui Dei essentiam, quatenus ut res extensa consideratur, certo et determinato modo exprimit*)."   But, with regard to that which is and acts within the body, this is but a mode or manner of existence which nature produces, which manifests itself in thought; it is not a spirit or a particular substance, any more than the body is, but a modality that expresses the essence of God, insofar as He is manifested, acts, and operates by thought. Have worse abominations ever been heard of in Christendom? Conceived thus, God cannot punish either the soul or the body, lest He punish and destroy Himself.

At the end of his twenty-first letter, he overturns the great mystery of piety, as it is touched on in I Timothy 3:16, maintaining that the incarnation of the Son of God is nothing but eternal wisdom, which, being shown generally in all things, and particularly in our hearts and souls, was ultimately manifest in an extraordinary way in Jesus

Christ. He says, a little further on, that it is true that some Churches add to that that God became man; "but," he says, "I have positively noted that I know nothing about what they mean by this" (*Quod quædam Ecclesiæ his addunt, quod Deus naturam humanam assumpserit, monui expresse me quid dicant nescire...*). He adds, "And that seems as strange to me as if someone advanced the idea that a circle assumed the nature of a triangle or a square." And, at the end of his twenty-third letter, he explains the famous passage in John 1:14: *the Word became flesh*, as a merely an Eastern colloquialism, saying that it only means that God was manifest in Jesus Christ in a completely particular manner.

In my sermon I have explained simply and, in few words, how, in his twenty-third and twenty-fourth letters, he tries to negate the mystery of the resurrection of Jesus Christ, which is our capital doctrine, and the foundation of our hopes and consolation. So, I will leave his impieties there.

SOME OF SPINOZA'S WRITINGS WHICH WERE NEVER PUBLISHED.

The publisher of *The Posthumous Works of Spinoza* names among the writings by this author which were never printed, a *Treatise on the Iris or the Rainbow*. I know of some people here in The Hague who saw and read this work, but persuaded Spinoza to suppress it; this may have upset him and led him toss it in the fire six months before he died, which is what his fellow tenants have told me did happen. He had also begun to translate the Old Testament into Flemish, and had conferred with experts in languages, informing himself on the Christian view of various passages. He had already finished the five books of Moses when, a few days before his death, he cast this book into his fireplace.

MANY AUTHORS REFUTE HIS WORKS.

His works had scarcely been published when God, for His own glory and the defense of the Christian religion, summoned various champions to refute them, which they carried off with all possible success. Doctor Theophilus Spitzelius, in his book *Infelix litterator*, names two of these authors: Frans Kuyper of Rotterdam, whose book, printed in that city in 1676, is titled *Arcana atheismi revelata*... ("The Deep Secrets of Atheism Unveiled"); the second is Regnerus van Mansveld, a professor at Utrecht who printed in the same city a book on the same subject in 1674.

In the following year, 1675, we see coming from Isaac Næranus's press, a book called *Enervatio, Tractatus theologico-politici*, a refutation of Spinoza's *Treatise,* by Jean Bredenburg, whose father had been an elder of the Lutheran Church in Rotterdam. Mr. Georg-Matthias Kœnig, in his *Bibliothèque d'Auteurs anciens et modernes*, p. 770, thought it suitable to name a certain weaver from Rotterdam: "textorem quemdam roterodamensem." If he was really one, I promise you that his book was the most capable and best one that any weaver ever wrote: his book demonstrates geometrically, clearly, and incontestably, that nature neither is nor could be God Himself, as Spinoza claims. Since his Latin was not up to scratch, he had to write his treatise in Flemish, and someone translated it into Latin for him. As he himself declares in the preface of his book, he wrote it to take away every excuse and pretext for Spinoza to claim such things, since Spinoza was still alive at the time of publication.

However, I find that some of this learned man's arguments don't carry water. Moreover, it seems that he inclines towards Socinianism in some places; that is my reading at least, although I believe I have the backing, here, of many enlightened people, and I will leave the matter in their hands. It is certain that François Kuyper and Bredenburg had various books printed against one another with respect to this Treatise, and that Kuyper, in his accusations against his opponent, claimed to do no less than to convict himself of atheism.

In 1676, Lammert Veldhuis of Utrecht published a treatise on ethics entitled *Ultrajectensis tractatus moralis de naturali pudore et dignitate hominis*, that is, "On the Natural Modesty and Dignity of Man." In this treatise he questions Spinoza's principles about where our ideas of good and evil come from; i.e. that they are produced by a superior and necessary operation of God or nature. I have already mentioned Johannes

Bredenburg, a merchant of Dort, who from 1674 onwards joined these ranks and refuted Spinoza's impious *Theologico-Political Treatise*. At this point I cannot help comparing him to that merchant of whom the Savior speaks in Saint Matthew, 8:45-6, since by offering his book to us, he is not giving us any worldly and perishable riches, but treasures of inestimable value which will never perish; and it would be much to ask that many merchants like him might populate the markets of Amsterdam and Rotterdam.

Our theologians following the Confession of Augsburg have also distinguished themselves by refuting Spinoza's impieties. His *Theologico-Political Treatise* had hardly seen the light of day when they took pen in hand to attack it. Doctor Musæus, professor of theology in Jena, deserves first mention: he was a man of great genius, perhaps unrivaled in his time. During Spinoza's lifetime, that is, in 1674, he published a dissertation twelve pages long, whose title was: *Tractatus theologico-politicus ad veritatis lumen examinatus* ("The Theologico-Political Treatise examined in Light of Good Sense and Truth"). He declares his aversion on pages 2 and for such an impious production, in these terms:

> The devil seduces a great number of men, all of whom seem to be on his payroll, devoted entirely to subverting what is most sacred. However, we may doubt whether any of them has been more effective than

100

this impostor at ruining all human and divine rights, who never aimed at anything but the ruin of the State and of religion.

Jure merito quis dubitet num ex illis quos ipse dæmon ad humana divinaque jura pervertenda magno numero conduxit, repertus fuerit qui in iis depravandis operosior fuerit quam hic impostor, magno Ecclesiæ malo et Reipublicæ detrimento natus:

On pages 5-8 he comments on Spinoza's philosophical propositions, pointing out their ambiguity, and showing plainly in what sense Spinoza certain words, in order to understand his thoughts as well as possible. On p. 16, § 32, he proves that Spinoza's ambition in publishing such a work was to teach that everyone had the right to form his own beliefs on matters of religion, and to restrict it only to those things which are within their reach and that they can understand for themselves. He had already, on p. 14, § 28, explained the issue perfectly, and pointed out where Spinoza deviated from Christian teaching; and in this way he completes his examination of Spinoza's *Treatise*, and no part of that book escapes his scrutiny. We must not doubt that Spinoza himself had read Doctor Musæus's book, since it was found among the belongings he left behind.

As already shown, although much has been written against the *Treatise of Politics and*

Theology, yet I would say that nobody did a more thorough job refuting it than this learned professor; and I'm not the only one who thinks so. The author who, under the name of Theodorus Securus, wrote a treatise entitled: *Origo atheism*, or "The Origins of Atheism", says in another short work entitled: *Prudentia theologica*, "I am quite surprised that Doctor Musæus's dissertation against Spinoza is so hard to find and so little known here in Holland; we owe everything to this learned theologian, who wrote on such an important subject, for he has certainly refuted it better than anyone." Mr. Fullerus, in Continuatione Bibliothecæ Universalis, etc., says about the same thing about Musæus "The illustrious theologian of Jena has roundly refuted the pernicious book of Spinoza with his usual ability and skill" (Celeberrimus ille Jenensium theologus Joh. Musæus Spinozæ pestilentissimum fœtum acutissimis, queis solet, telis confodit).

The same author also mentions Friedrich Rappolt, a professor in theology in Leipzig, who, in his inaugural oration, when he assumed his chair as professor at the university, likewise refuted Spinoza's views; although, having read his harangue myself, I find that the only goes at it indirectly without mentioning any names. It is entitled: "Oratio contra naturalistas, habita ipsis kalendis junii anno 1670"; and we can read it in the *Œuvres théologiques de Rappoltus*, V. I, p. 1386 and onwards, as edited by Doctor Jean Benedict

Carpzovius and printed in Leipzig in 1692. Doctor Johann Conrad Dürrius, a professor in Altorf, followed the same tack in a speech which I haven't read, to be honest, but which I am told is a very worthwhile contribution.

In 1681, Mr. Aubert de Versé published *L'impie convaincu; Ou Dissertation Contre Spinosa*[3], in which he attacked the foundations of this atheism. In 1687, Pierre Yvon, who was both related to and a follower of Labadie, and a minister in Leeuwarden, Friesland, wrote a treatise against Spinoza, which he published with this title: *L'impiété vaincue*, etc. In the *Supplément* to Moréri's *Dictionnaire*, in the article SPINOZA, mention is made of a "Treatise of the conformity of reason with faith (De *concordia rationis et fidei*)" by a Mr. Huet. This book was reprinted in Leipzig in 1692, and the journalists of this city have given reprinted a lot of it in the papers, in which Spinoza's ideas are very plainly exposed and refuted with great power and ability. The learned Mr. Simon and Mr. de la Motte, minister at the Savoy in London, have both written on the same subject. I have seen the works of these two authors, but my French isn't good enough for me to relate anything worthwhile about their books. Mr. Pierre Poiret, who is still living in Rijnsburg near Leiden, has supplemented the second edition of his book *De Deo, anima et malo*, with a

---

[3] *The Impious Man Convinced: Or, A Dissertation against Spinoza*

treatise against Spinoza, called *Fundamenta atheismi eversa, sive specimen absurditatis Spinozianæ* (The Principles of atheism overturned, etc.). This is a work that repays a careful reading.

The last one I will name is that of Mr. Wittichius, professor at Leiden, which was printed posthumously in 1690, as *Christophori Wittichii professoris Leidensis anti-Spinoza, sive examen Ethices B. de Spinoza*. It appeared shortly afterwards in Flemish translation and was printed in Amsterdam by Wasbergen. It is not surprising that, in a book which with a title like *The Sequel to The Life of Philopater*, the author would libel this learned man and soil the memory of the dead. In this pernicious book that excellent philosopher Mr. Wittichius is said to be a close friend of Spinoza's: that they nourished this friendship by many personal letters and conversations, that they held the same views, but that, wanting to defend his reputation as an orthodox Christian and keep himself free from any taint of Spinozism, Mr. Wittichius authored a book against Spinoza's *Ethics*, and waited until after Spinoza's death to publish it. These are this bold man's accusations; I have no idea where he got them from, nor what he bases his lies on. Where did he get the idea that these two philosophers had such a close relationship, to the point of visiting one another and exchanging many letters? Nobody has been able to find any letters written by Spinoza to Mr. Wittichius, nor from Mr.

Wittichius to Spinoza, either among his published or unpublished correspondence; so, we may conclude that this close relationship and their correspondence were pulled out of thin air by this liar. I never had a chance to speak with Mr. Wittichius, but I know his nephew Mr. Zimmermann pretty well; he is currently an Anglican minister, and he roomed with his uncle during his last years. He has told me the complete opposite of what the author of the *Life of Philopater* relates, and has shown me a letter he wrote at his uncle's dictation, in which Spinoza's ideas are both explained and refuted. Really, do we need anything more than his last book to clear his name? This book shows what his beliefs were, and it contains a profession of faith of sorts, and he wrote this shortly before he died. If anyone has any religious feeling at all, why would they dare to think, even less to write down, that all his books were sheer hypocrisy, put out just to let him keep up appearances, save face in the Church, and preserve him from some reputation as an impious man and a libertine?

Whether we may infer then that a correspondence was maintained between two people, seems unlikely to me; and I, like many other pastors, are wary of the same kind of accusations, since we cannot always avoid mingling with people whose beliefs are less than orthodox.

On this subject, I gladly remember Wilhelm

Deurhof, of Amsterdam, and name him with all due distinction. He is a professor who, in his works and particularly in his theological lessons, always attacked Spinoza's ideas fiercely. Mr. François Halma does him justice in his *Remarques sur la vie et sur les opinions de Spinoza*, p. 85, where he says that he had refuted these ideas so fully that none of his partisans has yet dared to engage or debate with him. He adds that this subtle writer is still doing battle with the lies on pages 193 of *The Life of Philopater*.

I will briefly mention two famous authors, and will join them together, although they are currently somewhat at odds with each other. The first is Mr. Bayle, too well-known in the Republic of Letters to require any praise here. The second is Mr. Jacquelot, previously a minister of the French Church in The Hague, and currently the court preacher to His Majesty the King of Prussia. Both men have written well-informed and good things about the life, writings, and ideas of Spinoza. What they have published on these matters, with the approbation of all, has been translated into Flemish by François Halma, a bookseller in Amsterdam and a man of letters. He has prefaced his translation with some well-placed notes about *The Sequel to The Life of Philopater*. His additions alone are worth the book's price.

It is not necessary to mention everyone who has written something against Spinoza's views since the book *Hemel op Aarden*, or "Heaven on Earth" by Mr. van Leenhoff, a Reformed minister in Zwoll; he is claimed to have built his ideas on Spinoza's foundations. These things are too recent and too well-known to spend any time on them, so I will skip them and proceed to this famous atheist's death.

There have been so many different accounts, many of which are quite apocryphal, about Spinoza's death that it is surprising that enlightened people have made such efforts to share such hearsay with the public, without taking due care to find out the truth. We find an example of such falsehoods in the book *Menagiana*, printed in 1695 in Amsterdam, where the author makes the following claims:

> I am told that Spinoza died from fear that he might be shut up in the Bastille. He had come to France, attracted by two persons of high quality who had desired to see him. However, Mr. de Pomponne, a minister who was very zealous for his religion, having been warned about this visitor, thought it unsuitable for Spinoza to visit France, suggesting that he might well excite disorder; to prevent this he resolved to have him thrown into the Bastille. When Spinoza was warned about his intentions, he saved himself by dressing up in the robes of a Cordelier; but I'm not completely certain about that last detail. What is for sure is that many people who have seen him have assured me that he was small, sallow, that he had something dark in his

physiognomy, and that he had the traits of reprobation in his countenance.

That is just a tissue of fables and lies, for Spinoza never visited France at any time; although some distinguished persons had tried to attract him there, as he told his landlords, however, he assured them at the same time that he was smart enough to avoid a mistake like that. As I will explain, he obviously did not die from fear. I will share the circumstances of his death objectively, and I won't make any claims without evidence; and I think I am in a good position to tell this story since it was here in The Hague where he died and was interred.

Spinoza's physique was rather feeble, unhealthy, and meager; he had also suffered with tuberculosis from the age of twenty. Thus, he was obliged to extreme sobriety in his choice of food and drink, and in his lifestyle. However, neither his landlord, nor any of his fellow tenants expected him to die so soon, and he was even surprised by it himself; for on February 22, which was the Saturday before Shrovetide, his landlord and landlady were in attendance at our church, listening to the sermon intended for a new communicant, whose ceremony will then be administered the next day, as is our custom. The landlord returned home after the sermon, four hours or so later. Spinoza had come down from his room and held quite an extended conversation with them, mostly about the sermon they had heard, and once he had finished his pipe he went back to his room, which was front-facing, and went to bed early. On Sunday morning before church, he came down again for a chat with the landlord and his wife. He had asked for a certain doctor from Amsterdam, whom I will only designate by his initials, L. M.; the doctor asked the tenants to buy an old cock and have it boiled straight away, so that Spinoza could drink its broth at midday, which he did, and took it with good appetite, and then the landlord and landlady went back to church. That afternoon doctor L. M. remained in the house alone with Spinoza, since everyone else had left as a group to attend the service. But when they returned home again, they were shocked to discover that at about three o'clock Spinoza had expired in the presence of this doctor, who, that very evening, returned to Amsterdam on the night-boat by night without taking the least care of the dead. He relieved himself from his duties immediately after Spinoza's death; and he seized a ducaton and whatever small change the deceased had left on the table, as well as a knife with a silver handle, and made off with this booty.

The details of his illness and death have been reported in very different ways by different authors; and this has given occasion for many debates. It is said: 1) that at the time of his illness he took precautions to exclude people who would only bother him; 2) that these very words came from his mouth several times: "O

God, have pity on me, a miserable sinner!" 3) that he had often been heard to sigh while pronouncing the name of God. This led those who were present to ask him whether, after all, he did believe in the existence of a God whose judgments he had every reason to believe after his death, to which he responded that he had only said it by accident. 4) it is also said that he had mandrake juice to hand, which he drank when he sensed the approach of death; that having then drawn the curtains of his bed, he lost consciousness, having fallen into a deep sleep, and then passed from this life into eternity; 5) finally, that he had expressly forbidden anyone to come into his room when the end was drawing near; as well as that, seeing the end coming, he had requested that his landlady forbid any ministers from coming to see him, because he said he wanted to die peaceably and without any arguments, etc.

I have carefully searched for the truth of these allegations, and repeatedly questioned his landlord and landlady, who are still alive, about them; both of them have consistently told me that they don't know a single thing about any of the above; they were of the opinion that all these so-called details were only lies, and that he never told them to refuse anyone whatsoever from coming in to see him. Moreover, in the end the only person with him in his room was the doctor from Amsterdam mentioned above; nobody could have heard his alleged plea: "O God, have pity on me, a miserable sinner!" And it seems unlikely that he ever really said such a thing, since he did not believe his end was quite so near, and his fellow tenants had no idea he was about to die. Also, he was not bed-ridden throughout his illness; for, on the very morning of his final day, he had already gone downstairs from his room as mentioned above; his room was the front-facing one where he slept in a bed made in the current "bedstede" style. The idea that he asked his landlady to refuse entry to any ministers who might show up, or that he had called on the name of God during his illness, is also unlikely since neither she, nor any of his fellow tenants, ever heard him, and they had known nothing about it. They are sure that he wouldn't have said such a thing, since after he had fallen victim to this illness he always kept up a truly Stoic resolve, even to the extent of reprimanding others when they complained a little too much during their own illnesses.

Finally, regarding the mandrake juice, which he was supposed to have taken at the end, which would make him lose consciousness, is another detail unknown to those who lived in the house with him. Now, these were the very people who prepared his food and drink for him, as well as the medicines he occasionally took. Neither does the apothecary remember anything about this drug, although he was the same man whom the doctor from Amsterdam had requested to bring the medicines Spinoza needed in his final days.

After Spinoza's death, his landlord saw to his burial. Jean Rieuwertz, a printer in Amsterdam, had requested this of him, promising to defray the expenses, since he had been hesitant about the cost. He wrote a long letter from Amsterdam on this point, dated March 6, 1678. In this letter he also mentions his friend in Schiedam, mentioned above, who showed how much he cherished Spinoza by paying exactly what Van der Spyck would have received from his now-defunct tenant. The sum he demanded was paid in full, as Rieuwertz himself had dealt with this matter on his friend's instruction.

When Spinoza's remains were about to be interred, an apothecary named Schroder raised an objection and demanded that he must first be compensated for the medicine he had previously furnished to the deceased. The cost of these was sixteen florins and two sous, as he remembered it; I find that this accounts for the saffron dye, the balms, powders, and so on; but there is mention of either opium or mandrake. This objection was quickly satisfied, and the casket and the other accounts were settled by Mr. Van der Spyck.

His body was set in the earth on February 25, in the company of many illustrious people, followed by six carriages. Upon returning from the burial, which was done at the Nieuwe Kerk on the Spui, some of his close friends and neighbors were regaled by several bottles of wine, according to the local custom, in the home of the deceased's landlord.

I will note in passing that Spinoza's barber gave, after his death, a memory in these terms: "Mr. Spinoza, of happy memory, owed Abraham Kervel, a surgeon, for having shaved him during the last quarter, at a cost of one florin eighteen sous." The prior ministering at the burial and two toolmakers paid the deceased a similar compliment in their memories, as well as the haberdasher who provided the mourning gloves.

If these good folks had been aware of Spinoza's views on religion, we may imagine that they would have been less eager to carry on as they did; or is it that they were merely following the normal custom, which sometimes allows such expressions of respect even to those who died without hope, or amid their final moments of impenitence?

Now that Spinoza was buried, his landlord had an inventory drawn up of his remaining movable goods. The notary's account of his role took this form: "Guillaume van den Hove, notary, having worked on the inventory of the furniture and effects of the late Mr. Benedict de Spinoza..." His fee added up to seventeen florins and eight sous; he noted that he had been paid in full on November 14, 1677.

Rebecca de Spinoza, the sister of the deceased, came forward as his heiress, and had this declared at the house where he died. However, as she had already refused to pay for his burial and to settle a few debts attached to the inheritance, Mr. Van der Spyck sent her to make her case to Robert Schmeding, porter of the procuration, in Amsterdam. The notary who set up this act and signed it on March 30, 1677 was named Libertus Loef. But, before paying a *sou*, she wanted to know for certain whether, once the debts had been settled, he would return what remained of her brother's goods. While she was deliberating, Van der Spyck got himself authorized to offer the goods and furniture in question for public sale, and then did so; and the proceeds were consigned to the normal place, and the sister of Spinoza stopped at that; but seeing that, after the payment of the fees and charges, little or nothing remained for her, she dropped her case. The procurator Jean Lukkas, who served Van der Spyck in this business, brought her the sum of thirty-three florins sixteen sous, of which he gave his quittance, dated June 1, 1678. His furniture was sold here at The Hague, on November 4, 1677, by Rykus Van Stralen, the sworn vendor, as per his account-book on that date.

You only have to cast your eyes over these accounts to realize that this was the sort of inventory that a true philosopher would leave; all it contains are a few notebooks, a few intaglios or stamps, a few bits of polished glass, some instruments to polish them, and that sort of thing.

These few tatters of his again show how frugal and domestic he was: a peddler's mantle with some briefs were sold for twenty-one florins fourteen sous; another gray mantle, twelve florins fourteen sous; four shrouds, six florins and eight sous; seven shirts, nine florins and six sous; a bed and a pillow, fifteen florins; nineteen necklets, one florin eleven sous; five handkerchiefs, twelve sous; two red curtains, a quilt and a little bed-sheet, six florins. His silver possessions consisted only of two silver buckles, which sold for two florins. The whole inventory or sale of the furniture only came to four hundred florins and thirteen sous; after deducting the fees and other charges for the sale, three hundred ninety florins and fourteen sous were left over.

Here is everything I have been able to learn about the details of the life and death of Spinoza. He was forty-four years, two months, and twenty-seven days old. He died on February 21, 1677, and was buried on the 25th of the same month.

Made in the USA
Coppell, TX
14 April 2021